"The sincerity, compassion and lov   , ur-
neys touches my heart more than words can express. . . . They each bring
a remarkable level of balance and joy into the world with their clients and
students and it is a joy to read their experiences."

—DENISE LINN, author of *Soul Coaching, 28 days to Discover Your
Authentic Self,* and Founder of Soul Coaching®
www.DeniseLinn.com

"I can easily imagine myself having a coaching session seated at Barbara's
cozy kitchen table with a hot cup of tea. Or, exploring the talents of a past
life with Irene. Or, bringing more soul into my work life using the methods
Helen employs with the corporations she coaches. *Soul Whispers* is a gift
to anyone who has stepped onto the path of inner discovery; those on a
personal journey towards healing, understanding and growth.

—DEB SWINGHOLM, photographer, Feng Shui
& Space Clearing Master Teacher
www.FloweringMoon.com

"*Soul Whispers* shares the depth, versatility and sheer possibility of Soul
Coaching as a tool that can give hope and healing to people everywhere –
regardless of their personal belief system. It is an expansive and uplifting
book with a beautiful mix of personal stories and technique – joyful and
refreshing to read!

—DEBORAH REDFERN, author of *Odyssey of the Heart,
Paths to Wholeness through Feng Shui,*
Master Educator of Interior Alignment® & Soul Coach™
www.DeborahRedfern.com

SOUL WHISPERS

Collective Wisdom from Soul Coaches
around the World

edited by Sophia Fairchild

FOREWORD BY DENISE LINN
Author of *Soul Coaching,*
28 Days to Discover Your Authentic Self

SOUL WINGS® PRESS
Laguna Beach, CA, USA
Sydney, Australia

Publisher's Cataloging-in-Publication data
Soul Whispers : collective wisdom from soul coaches around the world / edited by Sophia Fairchild ; foreword by Denise Linn.

   p. cm.
   ISBN 9780615290423
1. Self-actualization (Psychology). 2. Spiritual life—Anecdotes. 3. Personal coaching.
4. Life skills. I. Fairchild, Sophia. II. Linn, Denise. III. Title.
BF637.P36   F35 2009   158.1 21—DC22   PCN DATA AVAILABLE UPON REQUEST.

Excerpts from *Soul Coaching Oracle Cards Guidebook* by Denise Linn, reprinted with permission from the author and Hay House, Inc. Carlsbad, CA. Copyright © 2005 by Denise Linn.

All names have been changed to protect client confidentiality, unless otherwise noted. The authors of this book do not dispense medical advice or prescribe the use of any technique as a form of treatment for physical or medical problems without the advice of a physician, either directly or indirectly. The intent of the editor and authors is only to offer information of a general nature to help you in your quest for emotional and spiritual well-being. In the event you use any of the information in this book for yourself, which is your personal right, the authors, editor and the publisher assume no responsibility for your actions.

The terms Soul Coaching® and Soul Coach™ are Federally Registered Trademarks and remain the property of Denise Linn Seminars, Inc. Wherever the terms Soul Coaching® or Soul Coach™ appear throughout this book the appropriate trademark symbol is implied.

Editorial Supervision by Sophia Fairchild
Book Design by Fiona Raven

First Printing June 2009
Printed in Canada

Published by Soul Wings® Press
668 N Coast Hwy, Suite 234
Laguna Beach, CA 92651, USA
125 Oxford Street, Suite 125
Bondi Junction NSW
2022 Australia
www.Soul-Wings.net

This book is dedicated
with love and gratitude to
Denise Linn
who has always said
the soul loves the truth

Contents

Foreword

I'm sitting with my knees huddled tight against my chest. Out the window the sky is grey and threatening, and trees are thrashing violently back and forth. As I watch from the safety and warmth of my home, a wild wind careens through the valley that we live in. The big storm of the year has just started. Newscasters have been predicting this storm for the last week and warning to prepare for potential power outages. Branches of our 400-year-old oak trees are breaking and crashing down to the earth, as a piercing, cold rain is pounding the plants in my garden into a soggy, flattened heap of vegetation. The wind sounds like the howling banshees from the horror movies of the '50s.

And I'm celebrating . . . like crazy!

Why?

I'm delighted for a number of reasons. This downpour means the drought here is over. The rain that is now hammering our home— Summerhill Ranch—means that our plants will thrive through the dangerous heat of the coming summer months. This storm also means that the fire hazard here in the Central Coast of California will be diminished. (During drought years, fires sweep across the parched land here with a frightening fury.) Additionally, our water table is renewed so we don't have to worry about our well going dry.

I'm also exhilarated for another reason. Right before the storm hit, I finished reading this incredible collection of personal experiences and valuable information from Soul Coaches™ around the world, which you now hold in your hands. I was astounded at the width and depth of the journeys that these intrepid women have had in their Soul Coaching® profession. Their experiences range from a Buddhist retreat in the highlands of Thailand, to a Faery Quest in the Northwest wilderness, to a corporate training "with soul" in England, to past life journeys in the Scottish moors, to corporate executive miracles in Silicon Valley, to a "bad girl" rocking out in Toronto . . . and everything in between.

The sincerity, compassion and love that these women share in these journeys touches my heart more than words can express. It is said that it's a poor teacher whose students do not surpass his or her teachings; hence I must *not* be a poor teacher because these women have all gone beyond what I taught them in my professional certification Soul Coaching® course. They each bring a remarkable level of balance and joy into the world with their clients and students and it is a joy to read their experiences.

Well, the tempest is over, the skies aren't quite blue just yet but there's the freshness and vitality in the air that always accompanies the end of a squall. Just as this storm has refreshed the land, so each of these stories has refreshed my heart. It was a splendid gift for Soul Coach™ Sophia Fairchild to take such care to compile and edit these stories and to breathe spirit into this entire project.

It's an honor to be in this sacred circle of Soul Coaches™. I'm sure you will enjoy reading this collection of writings by professional Soul Coaches™ from all over the globe, as much as I have. Through their many voices, it's my wish that you too may hear the whispers from your soul!

Shimmering blessings,
DENISE LINN
Founder of Soul Coaching®

Introduction

$\mathcal{L}$ ike a labyrinth, the path of the soul is a spiraling journey, inwards to the central core of our being. This is the point of connection between all souls. Here, our soul's truth lies both hidden and expectant. From this most sacred place, our individual soul whispers messages to us through our dreams, magical synchronicities, and through all the encounters with meaningful people and events that appear on our path.

Our role is to pay attention to these small whispers, and to decipher their meaning, thus to discover and maintain true direction on our soul's path. This adventure sometimes requires overcoming fearful obstacles and life challenges that we ourselves have unconsciously created, and some that we did not. But in so doing, we may arrive at last at a place of peace and understanding, filled with a sense of deep belonging and communion with all of Life.

Constant whisperings and inner promptings from our soul steadily guide each of us on our life's journey. They not only help us to decide which destinations are most favorable to us, but to steer the fairest course. The Roman philosopher Seneca has said that "if a man does not know what port he is steering for, no wind is favorable to him." To take this analogy to its extreme, our decision about whether or not to pay attention to these whisperings can mean the difference between a fair and fruitful voyage, or getting hopelessly lost and founding on the rocks of despair.

Soul Coaching® provides a comprehensive system of deciphering these truthful and loving messages from our soul. This collection of stories and voices, gathered from all over the world, is designed to help steer you in your true life direction, one that will bring you the deepest meaning and greatest joy.

As Denise Linn explains, Soul Coaching is a remarkable program designed for anyone seeking phenomenal spiritual cleansing, renewal and transformation. Its aim is to align one's inner spiritual life with their outer life. It helps to clear away mental, emotional and physical clutter, so your client can hear the secret messages from his or her soul. It also allows your client to discover their true purpose, so they can design a life that supports that purpose.

Soul Coaching goes beyond the boundaries of ordinary life coaching which focuses on the attainment of goals. It is also not a type of emotional therapy. Soul Coaching is a guided inward journey to touch the sacred space within.

Each Soul Coach™ knows that their clients are naturally intuitive and resourceful, and understands that each client already has all the answers he or she needs. It is the job of the Soul Coach to create a safe, nurturing space for their clients to discover their own knowledge, while they listen with their heart as well as their ears. Soul Coaches work in several ways. They learn how to take their clients on inner meditative journeys called Soul Journeys to receive profound answers to heartfelt questions. They can also gently guide their clients through a 28 day program that is a deep inner and outer clutter clearing of the mental, emotional, physical and spiritual aspects of self, a journey represented by the Medicine Wheel and the elements of Air, Water, Earth and Fire.

As you will discover through the pages of this book, each Soul Coach brings to their professional practice a unique approach, some based on years of assisting others through complementary healing modalities, and others through personal expertise gathered from many different professional fields. The richness and diversity of knowledge and writing shared here is truly a feast. Feel free to sample and enjoy!

The chapters in your hands contain an abundance of insight and wisdom, laughter and learning, hope and joy to accompany you on your Soul Coaching journey. It is my wish that this book will inspire you to explore new approaches and techniques in your Soul Coaching repertoire that will not only deepen your practice, but will also give wings to your personal soul voyage.

May your journey through *Soul Whispers* be a true adventure for your soul!

SOPHIA FAIRCHILD
Sydney, Australia

BARBARA ROBITAILLE
Portland, Oregon, USA

OVER THE YEARS Barbara has often found herself sitting around her kitchen table, engaged in healing conversations with friends, neighbors and acquaintances. People are drawn to Barbara's table. Talk with Barb is quiet, gracious and graceful. With Barb conversation flows. As a Soul Coach™, Barbara offers gentle yet insightful observations that naturally bring to light each individual's own deepest wisdom.

A certified Soul Coach™ and Past Life Regression Coach through Denise Linn's Professional Soul Coaching® Course, Barb is also a Spiritual Response Therapy (SRT) Practitioner and Reiki Master. A former student of Sharon Turner's Awakenings clairvoyant training program, Barbara also draws on her natural gifts – compassionate listener, intuitive healer, skillful guide – and has set her professional Table to nurture others on their journeys of self-discovery, acceptance, healing and fulfillment.

Barbara Robitaille brings the conviction that our souls possess the wisdom to live fully. "Each of us is here to fulfill a unique destiny and to do so authentically and with joy."

Contact Barbara at Barbara's Table: Coaching Wisdom from the Inside Out at barbara.robitaille@gmail.com or www.BarbarasTable.com

Wisdom from the Inside Out

BARBARA ROBITAILLE

The invitation to come home to your Self can arrive suddenly.

My mother, the woman I had allowed to define my life, was dead; my father had died the previous year. After gathering the last of Mom's few belongings, my brother asked how I was. I responded that I had never felt freer in my life. Quietly nodding, he understood.

Suddenly, I had no one to disappoint, no one to tell me who I was or how I was to live. Always the good girl, I did as I was told and delivered all that they asked of me. I tap danced my way through life hoping to make their lives happy. There was love, but it was a hard love. As I watched my mother draw her last earthly breath, I felt the liberating breath of Spirit begin to awaken my Truth. I was forty-nine years old and only now gaining the courage to tell myself the truth about my life.

We never know the whole truth about someone's experience. Each of us has our own story, and, while we share our humanness with others, how we define ourselves and the situations we find ourselves in is uniquely our own. As a Soul Coach, I am privileged to listen to my client's stories. The power Soul Coaching brings you as the client rests in telling yourself the truth about your life. It's one thing to respond with "I'm fine" to a casual inquiry from a friend or neighbor, however too often we convince ourselves that we're fine when we're anything but. Too often we adapt ourselves to conform to the ideas, values and opinions of significant people in our lives: mothers, fathers, relatives, husbands/wives, co-workers, bosses, and we even adapt to cultural influences. At some point life brings you the opportunity to come home to yourself.

The invitation to come home to your Self can arrive suddenly; a phone call with news of a health crisis or the death of a loved one can, in a single moment, turn your world upside down. Sometimes the invitation arrives at one of life's thresholds, such as the experience of marriage, divorce, being a parent or caring for aging parents, empty nest, career transitions, or midlife. My invitation included all of the above in a matter of three years. It seems the Universe decided I needed to be hit by a thunderbolt to get my attention. It worked, but I wouldn't recommend it unless you have the budget for regular spa visits, the latest anti-aging skin care products and the right skin tone to compliment gray hair. What's true though is this – however the invitation is extended, feeling no solid ground beneath you, you stumble, looking for shelter with nowhere to go except home; to your Self.

Arriving at your own front door, luggage in hand, still indignantly waving the invitation, resisting the RSVP, you would rather be anywhere but here. Most of us would rather clean our refrigerator, scraping mold off cheese, tossing that stalk of broccoli bearing a striking resemblance to Bob Dylan, than choose to be alone with ourselves for longer than five minutes. Many of us are champion medal holders in creating distractions to avoid any time spent in quiet reflection. We keep ourselves distracted with volunteering to sew all the costumes for the school play or offering to return all our neighbors' library books. We make our lists and set our lives on cruise control, sailing smoothly along with only a minimal amount of self-reflection. We create a false sense of security, living on the surface choosing to ignore what lies beneath. As the busyness and stress we have created in our lives escalates we become disconnected from Spirit. But now the image in the mirror is unavoidable; it's time to go below the surface; unpack your bags.

As a Soul Coach I help you unpack. We examine the contents of each bag, and with honesty and intention assess what truly fits and let go of what no longer serves you. This might mean something as seemingly insignificant as letting go of that sweatshirt you wore at summer camp when you were twelve, along with Aunt Ruth's careless Thanksgiving comment when you were six, about your hair looking like a Brillo pad. As you do this, you begin to create space in your life. Composer Claude Debussy once said, "It is in the silence between the notes that true music is born." When you create space in your life, you welcome your Spirit home, you begin to hear the voice of your Soul, however soft the whisper, calling you to live from Spirit, to know your own Truth.

Soul Coaching offers the opportunity to reconnect to the voice of your Soul that knows what you love, knows what matters to you, knows who you want to be. You assess your life and in so doing tell the truth to yourself about your life. As you clear your mental, emotional, spiritual and physical clutter and reconnect with the natural world around you – the trees offering shade and music in the wind, the chickadees' cheerful song, the single flower that blooms through the sidewalk crack – you begin to open yourself to living a life guided by Spirit, awakening that part of yourself that has forgotten that we belong to each other and all life. I am humbled to witness my clients awakening to the magic and miracles that are a part of every minute of every day; seeing kindness in a stranger's eyes, hearing from a friend when you most need support, finding something that you thought was lost. They begin to discover just how extraordinary their ordinary lives are.

Those awakenings happen at my kitchen table. How ordinary is that? There is something comfortable and familiar about being at a table. For years I have welcomed people to my table where three beeswax candles glow on a bamboo mat. Friends, neighbors and strangers have found themselves sitting at my table telling me their stories. Over cups of tea, coffee, cocoa or sips of wine, the conversation that was waiting, happened. My home has always been my sanctuary; offering me a place to relax, create, feel safe and feel Spirit; a true shelter for my heart, mind and spirit. People felt comfortable at my table. There was an ease between us. Gently I would listen and counsel from my table. I never knew who might appear each day.

The time came when I left my kitchen table to set up shop in a *real* office as a Soul Coach. I was invited to join a local holistic health clinic and I agreed to become a part of a community that offered referral support and provided a sense of shared vision with colleagues. I honored my humble beginnings by naming my business Barbara's Table. Interesting energetic roadblocks kept coming up as I tried to set up my office space. Among the most memorable: being locked out on two occasions having been issued the wrong key, unable to disarm the security system, paint disappearing, and my phone unable to provide service. With each challenge I pushed forward, determined to establish myself in the mainstream career world.

Recently an "aha" moment opened my Spirit to what is true for me. Due to tricky appointment scheduling with a client, I agreed to see her at my home. I put the kettle on for tea and lit the candles in my kitchen – just like old times. The session carried the energy of ease and grace. I was in my groove! I was home. My intuitive gifts that I use in combination with the Soul Coaching program were at a heightened level and the intimacy of connection with my client felt deeper. She asked if we could meet in my home again the following week saying "I love being here." I knew without question that I was to come back to my table.

As we come back to ourselves, answering the question "Who am I, really?" our lives awaken to our wisdom within, hearing the soft whisper of our soul calling us to our truth, guiding us in bringing our light to the world. This is what it means to be alive; letting go of the fear that holds us hostage; having the courage to embrace the power to define your life; knowing you have the power to choose how you define each moment of your life. Howard Thurman once said, "Don't ask what the world needs. Ask what makes you come alive, and go do it. Because what the world needs is people who have come alive."

When you show up and make the commitment to dig down deep, it feels as though the Universe and your soul open floodgates to support you every step of the way, acknowledging the yearning that has been kept undercover, held captive by your ego and the mind that said, "You must do this if you want to be loved, if you want to succeed, if you want to belong." Grace descends and synchronicities expand. Those "aha" moments bring the gift of redefining your way of being in the world, transforming your life.

I have come to know and honor Mystery as I work with my Soul Coaching clients. Each day holds the promise of possibility and I never know which day's exercises or which Soul Coaching tool will be the one that will bring the delight of the "aha" gift of understanding and connection. For one client it might be

Day 9, examining the meaning we give to things, that brings them to their knees, another might resonate deeply with doing a Vision Board, where images, color or words hold the key to insights that awaken their Divine identity.

In cleaning out a closet recently, I found the Vision Board I made during my Soul Coaching training course at Summerhill Ranch. As I looked at it, I was stunned when I saw the words *Kitchen Table* pasted on my collage. My soul knew I belonged at my kitchen table. My ego took me on a detour, but my spirit brought me home. In the center of my collage there is an image of a woman standing on a stage holding a microphone. I remember feeling strongly drawn to that image and I get goose bumps as I stare at the image now, some years later, as I realize I now take voice performance lessons and own my identity as a singer.

With 28 days of powerful questions to reflect upon, meditations and hands-on tasks, the sense that anything can happen comes alive and opens the door to the Divine imagination within. Which Soul Coaching tool unlocks which door is different for everyone.

One of the most powerful tools used in Soul Coaching is composing a vow to yourself. In preparing to write this chapter, I contacted several former clients asking them what they found most helpful during their six week journey. Everyone included the writing of their sacred contract as one of the most meaningful tasks. As you might imagine, writing a vow to yourself, writing loving, tender, kind words brings a softening towards yourself that is unfamiliar, and uncomfortable. We're not used to being loving and kind to ourselves. Instead, the opposite is often the case. When we make a promise to a friend or family member we do everything possible to honor that commitment. Yet how easily we break promises we've made to ourselves. In writing a thoughtful, heartfelt vow to your self, you acknowledge your goodness, your shortcomings, and your strengths and make the commitment to accept and honor yourself.

Entering a Soul Coaching experience is like going on a holiday by yourself. This is a time when it's okay to say "It's all about me" – a time to allow yourself permission to focus on you, to ask yourself each morning "What do I feel like doing today?" and then doing it. You learn to keep promises to yourself. If you wake up wanting to go to Paris, and you know you won't be boarding the next plane to Charles De Gaulle airport, perhaps you could bring a little bit of Paris to your life that day – have a croissant and glass of wine for lunch at a local bistro, or spend time on the Internet looking up travel information to Paris. Print out a picture of the Eiffel Tower and create a Vision Board filled with other images or words you desire. The point is to take time to listen to your Spirit, to pay attention to your heart's desires; to nurture the childlike nature within, the part of you who remembers that magic happens.

There are many ways to open yourself to magic and miracles in your life. One way is to write down exactly what it is you desire and declare "I desire this or something better to come to me in perfect timing." A client of mine, Eric, decided to make a list of all the elements that, to him, created the perfect house. With no expected timeline, he put the list in a special box he kept on his dresser. Within two weeks, he received word that the condominium he was renting was being put up for sale. Rather than wait in uncertainty for the condo to sell, Eric began to look for a new place to rent. After viewing several options, he found a beautiful home in a neighborhood convenient to work and school. Upon inquiring, he learned that while he was welcome to make an appointment to view the property, there were over 100 applicants scheduled to meet the owner and walk through the house.

> ### Sanctuary
>
> *AFFIRMATION: I am divinely guided gently and lovingly.*
>
> *Go within and find your inner refuge. Be a safe haven for others. Step forward with grace, deliberation, and thoughtfulness. Take moments for reflection.*

Arriving at his scheduled time, Eric slipped in the front door, just as the couple before him was leaving. He overheard them offering the owner more money than she was asking for the monthly rent. Eric considerately removed his shoes as he entered the house and after exchanging a few pleasantries with the owner began to roam through the house. He loved the feel of each room, delighting in its quirky layout, knowing he would be at home in this place. Talking a bit more with the owner, he assured her of his genuine interest and desire to become her tenant. As the next couple arrived, Eric quietly left, knowing that while he felt good about his connection with the owner, many others were equally excited about living in this wonderful home.

Eric was chosen among all those who applied. He was ecstatic at his good fortune, but it wasn't until he had moved all his belongings and was settled in that he remembered his list. Smiling to himself he read his list of house desires, realizing that every single one of his desires was present in his new home. All except one. He had listed the desire for bamboo floors. The house did have hardwood flooring, but it was not bamboo. Later that day sitting in his living room, his gaze was drawn to the backyard, where, for the first time he noticed that his back fence line was planted entirely with – bamboo.

Self-care, acceptance and forgiveness are integral elements of the Soul Coaching experience. I challenge my clients to remember their manners toward themselves. We can be amazingly hard on ourselves. I had one client who made the decision to commit to the Soul Coaching program hoping to learn to say "Yes" to herself after a lifetime of self-cruelty. Growing up in a household where she was guilty until proven innocent, where nothing less than perfection was allowed, Emily apologized constantly and took the blame for whatever might go wrong, beating herself up for every little thing.

In our work together, we explored the words and tapes that played in Emily's mind as she made her way through the day. It is amazing how harsh and critical those inner voices can be. The judge and jury need to be dismissed and replaced with more compassionate and honorable voices. The good news is that you have the power to fire the judge and jury. Once the realization awakens, firing the judge and jury can be exhilarating! No need to mind your manners; let them go without two weeks notice – "You're outta here. Pack your things and get moving, *now!*" Bit by bit the new language emerges; the old tapes are erased and, as a result, decades of conditioned behavior can be redefined.

Many of us look back at events in our lives through a lens that blames others for our involvement or excuses our behavior. "The devil made me do it," the immortal line used by comedian Flip Wilson's character, Geraldine, to explain away her outrageous, mean-spirited behavior, was always good for a laugh, but not so funny when experienced off-stage. It's easy to blame our actions on someone else. But, it is important to own our actions, recognizing that we choose situations and how we respond in those situations, rather than adopting the position of being a victim of circumstances, blaming others, living in denial or making excuses.

One of the exercises in the Soul Coaching program, often the most uncomfortable for clients, involves looking back at your most memorable life experiences, those thresholds that you feel shaped your life from the position of being an observer – a Sacred Observer. Through the lens of the Sacred Observer, you detach from the emotional charge that you have used to define those moments, offering the opportunity for a new perspective that could assist you in seeing yourself in a new way.

Living your life from the place of being a victim holds you hostage; the hurts and wounds of the past remain alive in feelings of blame, denial, regret or fear, as well as robbing you of the future with the energy given over to worrying about future outcomes. You are not able to live in the present moment, to know the blessing of living this one moment, to rest in the space of *now.* Recognizing that you have the power to release living from a place of victimhood, that you are not a victim, knowing instead that you have the power to choose how you react or respond in any given situation is a huge step towards reclaiming and owning your power.

When you stand in your power, trust your own information and allow your intuition to guide you in making choices and decisions, life becomes truly your own. After years of wearing someone else's shoes you are now standing proudly and confidently in your own. You dance, sing, smile, laugh, cry and live from your Truth. You honor all that you are and open your authentic self to all that you imagine possible. You have come home to your Self, embracing your humanness and your Divinity. You *Believe.*

Years ago, I happened upon a letter written in 1513 by Fra Giovani[1] to a friend. The words in his note have echoed within me ever since. I offer them to you as a reminder that you Take Peace when you remember your connection to others and all life. You Take Heaven when you let go of past regrets and release worry about future outcomes; when you live in the present moment. You Take Joy when you awaken to the magic and miracles that are in every moment of every day. I believe Soul Coaching awakens you to the infinite possibility that is your life. You can choose to take heaven, to take peace, to take joy in your life. It is up to you.

I salute you.
There is nothing I can give you
which you have not,
but there is much that while I cannot give,
you can take.
No heaven can come to us
unless our hearts find rest in it today.
Take Heaven.
No peace lies in the future
which is not hidden in this present instant.
Take Peace.
The gloom of the world is but a shadow.
Behind it, yet within our reach, is joy.
Take Joy.

∽

---

1   Fra Giovanni Giocondo (c. 1433–1515) Italian architect, antiquary, archaeologist and classical scholar. Excerpt from A Letter to the Most Illustrious the Contessina Allagia degli Aldobrandeschi, Written Christmas Eve Anno Domini 1513.

SHERRIE ATAIDE
Chico, California, USA

SHERRIE'S LIFE JOURNEY is a continuous and wonderful unfolding of synchronicity, serendipity and signs. She has been led into several exciting careers; Human Resource Manager, Strategic Planning and Team Building Consultant, Director of a faith based non-profit, and Life Coach. Sherrie's passion is working with people who are interested in expanding their view of this magical planet we live on. Sherrie has created *Life Design* – a flourishing Soul and Past Life Coaching Practice. She also leads groups for those wanting to "step out of the box" to explore new ideas, and workshops for the expansion of personal and spiritual awareness and growth. Sherrie believes "each one of us has the answers to all of life's questions if we listen to the whispers of our soul". She provides a safe space to *listen for those whispers*. Sherrie lives in the beauty of Northern California where she follows her heart in this walk through life.

If you are interested in more information or connecting with Sherrie please write to her at ataide@aol.com or visit her website – www.LifesDesign.net

Synchronicity

SHERRIE ATAIDE

Be open to the whispers of your soul.

Synchronicity – a series of events the universe uses to guide us in creating what we desire and to provide answers to life's questions. These answers are always laid out for us. The key is to be open and receive.

A few years ago I found myself between careers without any idea of what I wanted to do next. Yet synchronicity was at play, gently guiding me toward becoming a Soul Coach through a series of magical events.

Not sure what to do with the next chapter of my life, for a few months I did nothing. I sat quietly with indecision. One day my dear friend Sherrill invited me to a lecture in San Francisco. I said, "Gee, I'd love to go but money is tight right now as I'm not working," which was a half truth. The whole truth was, even if I did have the extra cash the speaker wasn't my favorite. However, Sherrill was a bit more insistent and bought me a ticket to the event for my birthday!

Presented as a gift how could I refuse? I thanked her graciously, still thinking – gosh that's a lot of money to pay to hear someone I wasn't especially interested in. She said to me, "Sherrie, I really think you're going to find the direction you're looking for at this lecture." I still wasn't convinced but was willing to be open. We decided to make a fun weekend out of it and I knew it would be enjoyable to spend time with Sherrill if nothing else. On the three hour drive to San Francisco, Sherrill repeated with confidence her thought that this lecture was what I needed to gain the direction for my future work. I was surprised at her confidence about this.

The lecture site was packed with several hundred people. We found seats near the front, sat down and I listened intently, waiting for the words needed to define my future career. The morning went by quickly and we broke for lunch. Sherrill anxiously asked me, "Well, what do you think so far?" I told her I was pleasantly surprised, the lecture was better than expected and I was really enjoying it. She asked if there had been anything that might give me direction or ideas. I answered, "Not a thing." Sherrill wasn't put off by this and was still optimistic, "Well, we have the whole afternoon. I really think there's something here for you."

After lunch we returned to the conference area a bit ahead of the crowd. We sat sideways in our chairs talking to each other. Sherrill glanced back and saw a book on the seat directly behind me. She said, "Look, that looks like a book you'd be interested in reading." I turned completely around in my chair and saw a copy of *Soul Coaching: 28 Days to Discover Your Authentic Self*, by Denise Linn. I found the title intriguing. With a desire for personal and spiritual growth and exploration of new ways to know myself more fully, I made a mental note to buy the book and delve into it for more insights.

Upon returning home I immediately ordered the book. When it arrived I scanned it and in the back I read that Denise leads professional certification courses in Soul Coaching (the only one in the world!) I emailed the Institute and found it was just a few hours from my home and enrolled immediately. This was exactly what I was looking for, an amazing opportunity to learn to work with others in a spiritual and yet practical way. I knew right away this work was what I was meant to do. And so began my work as a Soul Coach. Sherrill was right; I needed to be at that lecture!

I believe these events were *divinely* inspired and came to me at exactly the right time in a way which no one could have scripted.

Let's look at these seemingly singular unconnected events for a moment:

- *I was unemployed.* I needed to be unemployed or I wouldn't have been thinking about a new career.

- *The person who lectured was a favorite author of my friend's* or she wouldn't have been interested in going.

- *I received my ticket as a gift* or I wouldn't have attended.

- *The lecture was held in a city close enough so that we could drive* or we wouldn't have been able to go.

- *We chose exactly the right seats out of approximately 400*, and sat in those seats sideways, or the Soul Coaching book would not have been seen.

- *Unknowingly someone brought with them a book that I needed to see* and which led me to Denise Linn and an amazing new direction for my life's work!

In her book, *Synchronicity – The Anatomy of Coincidence*, Carolyn North writes, "Whether we think of these coincidences as significant or as nothing but pure chance, we still feel a sense of wonderment, as if something a bit magical has just happened. And often it has." This is exactly how it feels! My life has been filled with these wonderful events that guide me to the next amazing step in my ever expanding journey!

So, what is synchronicity?
Carl Jung, the famous Swiss psychoanalyst, wrote that synchronicity is "meaningful coincidences" that describe concurrent psychic and physical events that

are connected and defy the probability of chance. Jung believed there is a realm beyond time, where mind, matter and spirit merge.

I use the term *synchronicity* to describe unplanned events falling into place to create amazing outcomes, usually in the most unexpected, fun and miraculous ways!

Over the years I've learned to watch life unfold with these hidden surprises waiting for me. It's always exciting when I pay attention. The amazing part is that the surprise is usually revealed in a way that could never have been imagined and I never know in advance which events will lead to great opportunity. So, saying "Yes" to life is important so as not to miss the seemingly random events that lead to an outcome beyond what you may have dreamed!

Many years ago while working as a Human Resource Professional for a Fortune 500 Company, the entire team of managers were involved in team-building exercises. 'Team-Building' was part of the fabric of Corporate America at that time. One exercise involved a series of questions that were to be answered individually and then shared with the rest of the team so that we would get to know each other on a deeper level, and then hopefully work more harmoniously. It was an insightful experience and at the end of the training I hung my *banner* of answered questions in my office.

Not long after, the corporation began to downsize and decided to close the location where I worked. In an effort to help over 200 employees cope with the inevitable loss of their jobs, the company called in Anne, a highly regarded therapist, to help manage the transition. Anne and I worked closely together during that time. One day she was in my office and saw the *banner*. She was intrigued by the concept of it and we talked about how the questions could be modified and used in workshops for personal growth! After the facility closed, Anne and I decided to try out our idea and get feedback from the participants. The Life Design Workshop was developed and all who came loved the opportunity for a creative way to look at their past, present and future and the workshop continues to be a hit!

Another great surprise that came from this synchronistic experience was that participants from several of the workshops wanted to continue their personal and spiritual work and requested that I lead a group. This Women's Group, as we call ourselves, has met monthly for eight years and is an amazing opportunity for us to explore new depths within ourselves and support each other on our individual life paths. Synchronistic events truly guide my life in a sacred way.

I'm continually surprised at how one event seemingly unrelated to the next is actually a wonderfully designed plan and if we simply go-with-the-flow of life without expectation of where it might lead, remarkable things happen!

"Strings of Synchronicities" is a term used in *The Power of Flow – Practical Ways to Transform Your Life with Meaningful Coincidence,* by Charlene Belitz and Meg Lundstrom. They say that "Synchronicities can happen one after the other, as though a point is being made over and over again."

That is what happened in Anna's story. Anna and Renee were childhood friends, living and playing across the street from each other. They grew up, married, had families and moved to different towns in central California. Years into their adulthood, Anna and Renee decided to coordinate the visits to their parent's homes at the same time so they could spend time with each other as well as their parents. They planned to take walks together and catch up on what was happening in each other's lives.

On their first walk Renee mentioned she was reading a book called, *The Seat of the Soul*, by Gary Zukav. Renee shared that it was really interesting and thought provoking. The name sounded somewhat familiar to Anna, she thought she'd probably heard about it on *Oprah*, but didn't think much more about it.

The next time they met, Renee mentioned that a friend of hers was planning to introduce the book at a Women's Group, where they would discuss the concepts and ideas at length. Renee asked if Anna was interested in going, though it would be a big commitment since the group met monthly and was three hours away. Anna asked again, "What was the name of the book?" She wanted to make sure that she wrote it down and checked it out before making a commitment. After their walk they said their good-byes with the intention that Anna would call Renee about the Women's Group.

> ## Opening
>
> *AFFIRMATION:* I am open to receiving the gifts of the universe!
>
> Be open to receive the gifts of the universe. There's nothing to fear, so allow your vulnerability to shine. Fling your arms to the heavens and exclaim, "I'm ready!" Stretch, expand, and venture forth: "Doors of opportunity are opening for you!"

Later that day Anna was with her family, at her sister's home, celebrating Mother's Day. When it was time to leave, Anna offered to drive her mother home as she wasn't feeling well. Anna gathered their belongings and headed to her mother's car. As she popped open the trunk she noticed that it was completely empty . . . except for one thing, *The Seat of the Soul*, by Gary Zukav! Anna was stunned. She asked where the book came from, her mother said "I have absolutely no idea." Anna said that was when she *knew* she was being led to the Women's Group. She'd been looking for a safe and supportive place to talk about spiritual matters. That's how Anna and I met!

Another way to experience the splendid order of the universe is once again described by Carolyn North, "Synchronicities, like falling in love, give us a glimpse – a peephole – into the very fabric of the Universe, its miraculousness and its utter simplicity, its ordered Wholeness and the wild shimmying of its ecstatic dance."

Kristi's story is a wonderful example of the miraculous workings of the Universe. When Kristi was in her late teens she was living with a girlfriend in a basement apartment. One afternoon they saw a pair of legs walk by the window of the base-ment living room. She said, "Hey, I know that guy, we work together." They ran upstairs to say "Hi." He said he was going to a friend's house just down the street and invited the girls to come over and hang out. They did.

Through this encounter Kristi met other friends and over time the circles of friends multiplied. However, one name came up repeatedly in these circles – Brian. "Oh, you've got to meet Brian, he's great!" "Hey, Brian will be here later, you'll really like him," and so on. This went on for a few years – but they never seemed to be in the same place at the same time. One evening Kristi went out with a girlfriend she hadn't seen in a very long time just to talk, catch up and have some fun. They were met later in the evening by her friend's boyfriend and his friend – Brian! After several years and countless opportunities that never seemed to materialize, they finally met.

They stayed up all night talking and discovered that they had been at the same concerts, parties, and football games, and on many occasions, only moments apart. They knew the same people, enjoyed the same activities, appreciated the same music, and shared the same sense of humor. They talked about all the times they could have met but never did. They talked until the next morning and have been together ever since! Several years later they married and now have a beautiful son.

They have reflected many times about how they had been so close so often and never met until the time was just right for both of them. Kristi believes the Universe (God) kept them near each other until they were both ready to embrace a loving relationship. Kristi says, "People come into our lives when we're ready, sometimes they are literally within arm's reach but it all comes together in God's time."

Signs also play an important part in the synchronicities of life. In her book, *The Secret Language of Signs*, Denise Linn writes, "When you think of someone and he or she calls, or you need something and it appears in your life, these are examples of synchronicity, and there is always a corresponding sign that goes hand in hand with the synchronicity. Sometimes the sign is saying that you are expanding your horizons beyond the material physical plane. At other times the sign is giving you a profound look at your inner spiritual path. Pay particular attention to the signs that come to you through synchronicity."

Tina's story is a perfect illustration of how signs appear to validate or cheer us on in the direction that is for our highest good. Tina was struggling with whether or not she was on the right path. She had separated from her husband and was trying to build a new life. Questions swirled in her head – would it be better for her young son and an easier life for her just to reconcile, or continue to do the hard work and stand on her own? Finances were meager and she struggled with the idea of placing her little boy in daycare fulltime so that she could find a better paying job, or she wondered if should she do what her heart was telling her and try to find work that would allow her son to be with her. These were big life-changing decisions to make and there were times she was filled with doubt. One night while praying she asked for a sign that she was on the right path. Life was hard and she wanted something to tell her she was headed in the right direction, so that some of the confusion and emotional struggle would lift. The sign she asked for was a heart – just something in the shape of a heart.

Not long afterwards, Tina was cleaning house, still feeling scared and confused. She was thinking that she didn't know how the bills were going to be paid, wondering whether she was making the right choices, how was she going to make it all work. She was washing the bathroom wall and in so doing removed a small shelf – she just stood there with the shelf in her hand, a bit stunned. The plaster around the nail where the shelf had hung fell away in the perfect shape of a heart! She was excited and doubtful all at the same time. She called me right away and asked if she was making more out of this than she should. I said, "Don't doubt it, you asked for it a sign and it came." Tina began to relax into knowing that her prayer had been answered. She was sure that no matter how difficult it was at times, she was on the right path.

Since this experience, Tina receives hearts in the most unusual ways and during the most difficult times. Not long ago Tina was involved in a legal case. She was trying so hard to understand how and why this was happening to her. Should she continue to stand in the truth, as difficult as it was, or give in and let the whole mess go away? Doing the right and truthful thing can oftentimes be the hardest thing to do. She was on a trip to San Francisco with family and they stopped to have lunch. Tina was pretty distraught over the court case which involved her ex-husband and son. Once again, she needed guidance about the path to take; give in or fight for the truth? After lunch her son went outside with his Aunt to wait for the others. He was standing by the restaurant sign when he looked down and saw a small sparkling glass heart. He thought it was *cool* and wanted to show his mom. He went back inside the restaurant and handed it to her. She began to cry. It was exactly what she needed and once again *knew* she was on the right path. She continued to fight for the truth and was victorious.

Tina interprets her hearts as God communicating with her in their own special language! She is always grateful and says "Thank you" each time one appears in her life. Tina has created a beautiful and soulful life. She lives in the knowledge that the universe provides what she needs – when she asks.

The Dalai Lama said, "I am open to the guidance of synchronicity, and do not let expectations hinder my path." I believe this to be a key practice in being present in our lives and allowing the universe to guide us.

Looking back over the years, synchronicity has been the most significant factor in bringing me to where I am today. Early on I didn't always recognize the guidance of the universe, and occasionally may even have cursed a particular life experience until I was on the other side of it and could see the bigger picture and understand what a blessing the sequence of events really was.

All you need for the miracles of synchronicity to play out in your life is to be

OPEN to the gifts and guidance that God, the Universe, or Life (which ever word you choose) has for you. Open your mind and your heart and say "Yes" to life.

Ask for guidance - simply ask for what you need or want and the answer will always come. Ask in prayer or meditation, ask in journaling or visualizing, ask in thoughts and conversations, and ask while walking in nature. Then be open and allow the answer to come to you in surprising and mysterious ways.

Be open - make a point to be open to the whispers of the universe by taking nothing for granted. A leading authority in creative thinking, Edward de Bono, invites us to "think sideways." Be open to messages that come to you through signs, music, people, events, numbers, and nature. Watch and listen to all that is happening around you. What might the Universe be saying to you? Look for Divine guidance.

Receive - allow the answer to be what it is. Follow the nudging of the universe. Don't try to rationalize it or dismiss it. Follow your intuition and feelings with no preconceived expectations.

Give Thanks - live in a state of gratitude, for all of life is a wonderful gift. Gratitude allows us to be open to all that awaits us. Give thanks for where you are in each moment and know there is Divine guidance into the next moment. No need for worry, just appreciate the synchronicities of life.

May you embrace divine synchronicity in *your* life.

A heartfelt *Thank You* to members of my Soul Family for sharing their stories.

～

Bibliography

Belitz, Charlene & Lundstrom, Meg. *The Power of Flow – Practical Ways to Transform Your Life with Meaningful Coincidence:* Three Rivers Press, 1998.

Linn, Denise. *The Secret Language of Signs – How To Interpret The Coincidences and Symbols In Your Life:* Ballantine Books, 1996. (Formerly titled *Signposts: The Universe Is Whispering To You*)

North, Carolyn. *Synchronicity – The Anatomy of Coincidence:* Regent Press, 1994.

Further Reading

Cousineau, Phil. *Soul Moments – Marvelous Stories of Synchronicity – Meaningful Coincidences from a Seemingly Random World:* Conari Press, 1997.

Hopcke, Robert H. *There Are No Accidents – Synchronicity and the Stories of Our Lives:* Riverhead Books, 1997.

Upczak, Patricia Rose. *Synchronicity Signs & Symbols:* Synchronicity Publishing, 2001.

CAROL DAIGNEAULT
Rockport, Maine, USA

DEVELOPING AND SHARING a *new view* has been the focus of Carol's life work. For many years she marketed her creative wares, original watercolors and jewelry through her New View Studio while also studying and practicing personal empowerment techniques. Fourteen years of experience with an intuitive development study group continues to be one of her most treasured activities.

Later, she integrated her passions and established her current endeavor, New View Interiors, which offers Feng Shui, interior redesign and intuitive development services. "Throughout my life I was interested in what appeared to be two entirely different arenas – art and design and personal empowerment. When I read my first Feng Shui book I was thrilled to realize how naturally the two worlds blended together."

Earning certifications from the Western School of Feng Shui and Graceful Lifestyles Interior Redesign Program enhanced her natural abilities. The next step was her Soul Coaching® Certification.

Carol has worked as a Feng Shui practitioner for many years with individuals and small businesses, many in health care. Helping others to live a more fulfilled life is always the focus of her work. "My intent is to empower, educate and assist clients to realize their own place of harmony – to develop a new, more expanded view of themselves and their environment." She augments this vision by offering a monthly intuitive development circle.

Carol is available for Soul Coaching® and Feng Shui consultations and workshops. Please visit her website, www.CarolDaigneault.com, for additional information.

Modern Day Alchemy

CAROL DAIGNEAULT

Love it, use it or get rid of it!

I looked around the storage room over my garage and sighed. Although I had cleaned it several times since our move into this house six years earlier, the remnants of a distant past still stared back at me. Rusted Tonka toys, a broken toboggan, my children's red wagon and a weary air hockey table remained tucked into the eaves in the same spots they had been placed the day we put them there. My plan of saving them for the grandchildren had not yet materialized. Though my two sons were now twenty-nine and twenty-five and one was married – no babies were in sight. Why would I want my future grandchild to play with these weary, dust laden relics anyway? Sentimentalism, pure and simple. I clearly remember that my mother-in-law had given my young boys a shiny metal truck and trailer that had been their father's. I dreamt of continuing the tradition. However, the toys in my garage were not shiny, let alone safe.

I grabbed the trucks and carried them downstairs to start a pile to bring to the dump. We would never use the miniature air hockey table, so down it went. But, could someone else use it? I decided to start another pile – a give away pile. After all, I still had the two plastic paddles and it only needed one minor repair; maybe my cousin, who was handy, would want it for his eight year old son.

Back at the top of the stairs, I surveyed the mess. My old microwave still worked so perhaps the local Swap Shop would want it. Items in good working order could be donated there for others to pick up for free. This was certainly recycling at its best, "Save the Environment" and all that. Down it went.

We'd completed a remodeling project a few months earlier and the carpenters had left a door frame in the garage that had somehow managed to find its way upstairs. "Hmmm, we could take it apart and saw it up for kindling," I thought . . . "No," I told myself, "be strict!" Down it went. I felt myself really getting into this process. I puttered and pondered, climbing up and down the stairs for another hour. Two big, beautiful piles of cleared clutter were the result. This was great; things were coming together! Feeling quite satisfied with myself, I called to borrow my mother's pickup truck. I wanted to keep my momentum going.

As a Feng Shui practitioner in addition to being a Soul Coach, I had recommended clearing out the clutter many times to my clients and had seen remarkable out-comes from their efforts. There was a particular goal I was pursuing, but my focus on it was sporadic. I had decided to write a personal memoir and, although I had initially made progress with it, I now felt stalled on the project. Words like *stalled, stuck, congested* and *blocked* when used to describe how you feel are signals to look further. The environment you live and work in holds clues about the flow in your life. Since I felt stuck, I looked for places in my home that felt that way to me; this sent me on a search for places that held long-term storage and that led me to the congested stashes of old belongings tucked away in the upstairs room of my garage.

The next morning I continued my adventure with the borrowed truck brimming. Since I live in a relatively rural part of Maine, we have a dump where five different towns bring their trash. Twenty years ago we were allowed to back up to a large hole there and toss whatever we wanted into it. Today the facility is officially called the Five Town Transfer Station and requires quite a bit more attention and perse-verance to visit than it used to. Rolling to a stop at the gatehouse, I was greeted by a friendly yet official looking gentleman. Before I could ask him for directions to the Swap Shop he sauntered off on a casual stroll to the back of the vehicle.

"The door frame goes to the construction debris pile, the microwave to the appliance hopper, the old metal to the scrap metal area. Go see if she'll take the other stuff at the Swap Shop and, if not, put it in the dumpsters," he directed with the stoic abruptness often found in Maine. My brain started to spin. *Metal, wood, hopper . . . where?* Oh dear. I should have paid a trash pickup service to take it all away for me. My upper lip started to sweat as I began to feel anxious. *I can do this*, I prompted myself. Grinding into first gear I headed toward the Swap Shop.

A charming little wooden shed, the Swap Shop looked quiet. I pulled up and sheepishly looked around. A couple was inside examining some glass figurines. Bravely, I grabbed the dull garden clippers I was ready to part with. As if by magic the woman in charge of screening my obviously superior, and soon to be treasured, items appeared.

Let me be perfectly clear, I was in no way trying to pawn my useless junk off onto the unsuspecting citizens of my community. From the depths of my envi-ronmentally friendly heart I felt that all of these items were intrinsically useful. I could have had one heck of a yard sale and kept all of the proceeds for myself but, no, I was willing to share.

The Swap Shop attendant proceeded with the ceremonial stroll around the vehicle. Being a bit more thorough than the previous gentleman, she dug into the bed of the truck to see what was lurking in its depths.

"I can take the Tonka trucks and maybe those clippers," she said.

I waited. She began to turn to walk away. *What?* I objected in my head. This was an entire garage full of valuable items and she was turning them down?

"What about the toboggan?" I asked.

"Anything broken on it?" she pressed.

"Only one board on the bottom," I mumbled, defending my position. I reasoned to myself that it would be easy to fix. Wouldn't someone handy, like my Grandpa was, love to fix it? I looked around but didn't see any *Grandpas* in the area hungry for a project.

"The air hockey game even has the paddles," I added, beginning to feel like a used car salesman who was kicking the flat tire of the car she was trying to unload.

"Nobody seems to want those kinds of games anymore. We can't get rid of them," she countered.

Yikes! I thought. Do these spoiled kids today only play their fancy video games? Pleading, I persisted.

"How about these nice laminate bookshelves? They're almost brand new."

"You can leave them there and we can see," she acquiesced.

I think she had started to feel my desperation. She was probably accustomed to us would-be environmentalists trying to unload our unwanted possessions onto the public. Reluctantly I picked up my four items.

A bit downtrodden, off I went to the construction debris pile. Large, wooden items are disposed of here. Wrestling the door frame from the bed of the truck, my attempt to heave it onto the pile resulted in my dropping it about three inches from my feet. "Good enough," I concluded. Tiptoeing toward the truck I made the mental note to never wear sandals to the dump again.

Now, moving on to the appliance hopper, the first word that came to my mind was, "astonishing." It was a graveyard for old metal microwaves, stoves, refrigerators, sinks and I am not really sure what some of the other things left in the pile even were. Again I reasoned with myself about the value of my clutter. My microwave worked, perhaps at half power, but it was still good. It didn't heat well enough for me to keep it but wasn't there some poor soul who could use it, perhaps a non-profit group? Alas, no, so out it came. "Whoa!" I thought. Who knew a fifteen year old microwave weighed at least 150 pounds? Despite its bulk I did manage to actually get it in the hopper, but the sound of glass breaking as it hit the pile was truly grizzly.

I finally conceded that everything else in the truck was, indeed, trash. So, I backed up and drove over to the cavernous dumpsters that are later trucked off to an incinerator. Heading for the exit, I glanced toward the Swap Shop. My spirit soared as I saw a man with a big smile walking away with the Tonka trucks in

---

Simplicity

AFFIRMATION: Deep, profound serenity is expanding in my life!

Do what matters; and release the rest to find peace, grace, and stillness. Clear internal and external clutter.

his hands. "See," I thought, "I knew someone could use some of my great stuff." I drove away feeling victorious!

The bed of the truck was empty but the entire cab was still full of useable clothes and household items I wanted to give away, so I steered toward our local Goodwill store which raises funds for various projects by selling donated items. Happy to find a parking space up front, I began unloading, looking over my shoulder to see if anyone was coming to censor my generosity. "Maybe they are all at lunch?" I reasoned. All four loads were inside before a smiling clerk inquired about whether I was making a donation.

"Yes, yes, all of it, thank you." I held my breath.

"Would you like a receipt?" she inquired.

"Well yes, I would!"

Now this was the way to treat someone with good stuff like mine! My tax deduction donation form in hand, I almost wept with joy as I returned to the empty truck. *Seldom do any of us achieve so much in such a short time.*

If I said to you – clear your clutter and there will be a shift in your life – would you think that statement was: Crazy? Too easy? Ridiculous? It won't work? Well, I absolutely know it works because it worked for me. Figuratively, or energetically, releasing this clutter had begun an unpredictable shift in my life. Denise Linn calls clutter clearing "Modern Day Alchemy"[1] and that is what this adventure produced for me. My writing took off. Although totally inexperienced as a writer, the opportunity to participate in this book almost magically manifested. Thinking I could write a brief one to two page story, I was surprised to be asked to contribute an entire chapter.

A basic principle of Feng Shui is that everything is alive with ch'i.[2] Ch'i is vital energy and it permeates every bit of your clutter, giving each item its own life and capacity to interact with you. One piece of wisdom passed down through generations of Feng Shui practitioners advises that: *Your stuff is talking to you all the time, make sure it has good things to say.* When the negative, stressful messages of our clutter are removed, old stuck energy is removed as well. This allows fresh, new ch'i to flow in and more positive circumstances are able to emerge. Do I really think cleaning up the garage created opportunities for me, and it wasn't just a coincidence? Absolutely, because I've seen the lives of many others change after they have done clutter clearing.

My oldest son spent a few hours emptying boxes of items he had left behind in our basement after college. All were childhood mementos such as swimming medals and trophies, souvenirs from school trips, t-shirts, CD's and books. When he had undertaken this project he'd been less than excited about his employment. Within six weeks of clearing his childhood clutter he had been transferred to a new department and into a position he found much more fulfilling.

1   Linn, Denise. *Soul Coaching.* Hay House, 2003
2   Collins, Terah Kathryn. *The Western Guide to Feng Shui: Room by Room.* Hay House, 1999

Clients of mine had a large tree that had fallen in their yard after it was choked by bittersweet vines. Note: clutter isn't simply inside the house. After clearing away the debris and landscaping the area there was a breakthrough in the family. Their adopted daughter was offered a treasured family heirloom by the grandmother who had seldom acknowledged her before. In a further example, another client, a twenty-something young man, found several items stored away that were reminders of an old girlfriend. He let go of photos, stuffed animals and even a jar of sand from the beach by the old beau's childhood home. Although he had barely dated in the three years since their breakup, within two months of clearing these items he was in a very serious new romantic relationship.

Once you experience how clutter clearing impacts the flow of energy in your life you may be inspired to do it all the time!

Why do we accumulate clutter?

In the case of my garage, it was sentimentalism and the difficulty of separating from the past in regards to my sons' childhoods that was my reason for hanging onto items. There was some inherited clutter – the items left behind that I no longer wanted but thought my kids might want to have for their adult homes someday. Another big factor was indecision on my part. I just needed to figure out what to do with some of these items, and that invariably stalls the process.

Do you trust the Universe or yourself to be able to provide for your basic physical or emotional needs? Many people hold a lifelong fear of not being able to take care of themselves and thus they accumulate stuff around them to make them feel more secure and prepared for what lies ahead. Often, people don't fathom the volume of things they have held onto. They may not understand that their excess stuff is holding them back rather than providing the financial security or emotional support they crave.

Other people build clutter as a response to stress or overload by not having the focus or time to sort and organize. However, this pattern can go on for years without being addressed and often the clutter takes over and perpetuates the imbalance. This would be a good time to rally outside help by hiring a professional organizer.

In all cases I'd say that the cart comes before the horse, or, the underlying belief comes before the clutter. In Week One of Soul Coaching we are asked to examine some of our core beliefs and begin to clear out those that don't support who or what we want to be in the world. Done in conjunction with physical clutter clearing, the results can be powerful.

How do I know if it's clutter?

Tidy people sometimes don't realize that their homes are loaded with clutter. Clutter is anything you don't love or don't use, period. If you don't love it and will never use it, it doesn't matter if you got it for free, your relative gave it to you for a gift, it just needs a little fixing, it was a bargain, it cost a lot when you bought it, it will come back into style some day or it is still as good as new. When any of these phrases can be applied to an item, it is definitely clutter – Love it, use it or get rid of it!

It seems *so* overwhelming. How *do* I even start?

One friend told me that it is actually painful for her to clutter clear. Another mentioned to me that she knows that she is being held back by her clutter but hasn't been able to motivate herself to start clearing yet. Do not beat yourself up. Ask yourself – can you start small? One square foot of the bathroom counter, one stack of magazines or one row of a bookshelf are all manageable projects, for example. Allocate ten minutes to the project – sort for five minutes and then clean up and throw away for five. Leaving things looking better than when you started is important.

Clutter clearing is a new skill many need to learn. Most of us have practiced to know how to cook or operate our electronic equipment. Clutter clearing is a similar skill that helps you to keep your life running smoothly. If you need more than my instructions or what various books offer, consider partnering with a friend and working one morning at your house and one morning at hers.

Once I decide to move ahead, how do I actually remove the clutter?

My experience cleaning the garage is a good example of how to organize the adventure of clutter clearing. The method I used was to sort the items into 3 – 4 categories. Your piles could include:

Sell ~ Yard sale, e-bay, auction and consignment are a few ways to cash in on items that have more substantial value. If you're not interested in pursuing this avenue, shift these items to the next category.

Donate or give away ~ Items that are in good working order and have some worth are potential gifts to charities, schools and religious organizations that are often happy to accept them. Visit my website, www.caroldaigneault.com, for ideas of places to donate or dispose of your items. Give away an item only when you know it is *perfect* for a relative or friend and you are willing to deliver it directly to them. It is imperative that you are mindful that you aren't simply passing it off to them and adding to their clutter.

Recycle ~ Our dump takes metal, newspaper, magazines, everyday paper and certain plastics. Inquire with your local municipality for their recycling guidelines. Some folks take items from the "sell" or "donate" pile and recycle them as gifts.

Throw away ~ You will definitely discover things that are trash, pure and simple. It will feel great to throw them away!

What if I am undecided about a specific item?

Pay particular attention to the feeling the item brings up for you. If you rediscover something buried under a pile and are elated you found it, it's probably a keeper. However, if an item elicits negative feelings such as guilt or reminds you of what bad taste your sister-in-law has, it's best to let it go. Our stuff does act as an environmental affirmation for who we are. Be sure it is a positive affirmation by eliminating all of the items around you that remind you of past difficulties and stresses and, therefore, may hold those negative memories in place for you now.

In particular, be wary of keeping items that remind you of major life challenges such as divorce and breakups, deaths, illness or old jobs left on a bad note. These items hold the energy of those past situations and may connect you to the negative memories when you encounter them. If, when you see an item, it conjures up uncomfortable recollections of the event or associated people involved, it would serve you well to remove the item from your environment permanently.

The Grande Finale!

Once you have your boxes or piles all set, it is crucial to quickly get them to their new homes; boxes full of sorted clutter are still clutter so complete the process! For many people, this is the most challenging part.

Bonus Points – looking for results

I expect noticeable life enhancing results when people clutter clear. First, you have the satisfaction of seeing the clean, organized space emerge. Second, you should begin noticing new opportunities and possibilities coming your way because you've made space for them. Many of my clients have reported that, at this point, they experience more synchronicity, insights and opportunities – they start hearing the wisdom of their soul more fully.

Soul Coaching

The aim of Soul Coaching is "to align your inner spiritual life with your outer life."[3] One of the primary tools of Soul Coaching is clutter clearing which asks you to remove environmental distractions and blocks. With the clarity this provides you can start receiving higher guidance by beginning to notice the messages of your soul.

I tell my clients that our ultimate goal is to have every part of the home or work environment elicit a reaction of "Oh! I love that! It makes me feel so good." That is a goal worth striving for. I know it is possible because that was my reaction when I visited Denise and David Linn's incredible home, Summerhill Ranch, for my Soul Coaching training. I don't offer this goal to set unreasonable standards but to invite you to embrace the environment around you and organize it so it is a partner in your personal growth.

As Denise Linn says, it's "modern day alchemy."

∽

---

3   Linn, Denise. *Soul Coaching*. Hay House, 2003

ROBERTA ASHKAWA BINDER
USA

ROBERTA ASHKAWA BINDER has been working with amazing clients internationally as a Decisions Coach since 1991 when she graduated from the VITA Certification training. In 2004 she attended Denise Linn's Soul Coaching® Certification and is now able to add an additional level of coaching and a new collection of tools for clients' new-skills-toolboxes. In fall 2008, she completed a three year Shamanic apprenticeship, and incorporates the ceremony and peace-filled insight of this knowledge into her practice.

As a resident of Earth Mother, Roberta and her two cats, live in a comfy little home in the United States. A busy editor, she frequently can be found (in the warm weather) sitting on the banks of a local river or stream working on her latest project – oh the glories of laptops! Roberta is active in the educational programs of her home church, teaching classes and workshops; she is also a frequent guest facilitator for women's retreats in other churches.

With a growing local and international client base, she travels several times a year providing workshops and seminars throughout the United States. If you would like to schedule a coaching consultation, workshop, retreat, or have a project that needs editing, you can reach Roberta at www.EvolvingChoices.com or www.RobertaEdits.com

Decision Circles

ROBERTA ASHKAWA BINDER

*Decisions are the commitments we make on a soul level
that reveal our Spiritual Truths.*

When I took my Interior Alignment® Feng Shui and Seven Star Blessing Space Clearing Certification course with Denise Linn in San Luis Obispo California in 2002, Denise announced to us that this was the last class she would be teaching. She was moving on to a new program she had been exploring, and was now ready to devote all of her time to a 28 Day Program called Soul Coaching. She went on to tell us that she was in the process of writing a book and invited any of us who were interested to explore with her the initial program.

Since I was already a Decisions Coach, with over twenty years of experience, this seemed like an exciting opportunity to augment that material with some fresh new ideas. So I signed on for the first trial run of Soul Coaching. Even at this early stage, I could see the potential benefits for my clients of combining this new program with my Decisions Coaching practice and later, became a Certified Soul Coach.

Decision Coaching/Mentoring

The Decisions program enables clients to recognize the decision circles they repeatedly get themselves into, and to experience how to break destructive decision habits by recognizing how and why they happen, then move into more positive and constructive decision skills. Often these new skills are life changing experiences. It also supplies them with a new toolbox of actions and reactions to call on when potentially negative decision situations surface.

Studies show that our decision making skills are developed in infancy. Babies' brains do not come fully wired; we all arrive with brainstem knowledge and the rest is a learned process. This is the reason that the earlier a baby is stimulated with simple and on-going learning experiences, the more full-brain learning and function is completed. This learning begins with the early cuddling, cooing, lullabies, story-telling, and sensory stimulation that is generally natural to parents. If missing, we've all seen the pictures of babies left with no human touch in silent wards of over-crowded orphanages.

Cognitive cause and effect primarily is set within the first two years, so circular

patterns of negative decision cycles that can last a lifetime are established as toddlers. Providing infants with early choices of no more than two items is the beginning of the toddlers' decision making process, and when the infant's decision is
rewarded with the object of choice, positive learning begins.

Consider Hank who was in his early forties. He had been cycling in and out of
prison since his teens. Hank had grown up on the rough side of town and although
his was a two parent family, he was left on his own from a very young age. His
negative decision making cycle started with petty theft, and as he got older those
crimes landed him in prison. However, rather than learn his lessons and make
more positive decisions, each time he was released from prison, the crimes grew
more daring and the sentencing longer.

When Hank and I first met it was as part of his parole requirement; he had
been identified as well on his way to a life in prison, without more clearly defined
cognitive skills. The parole board's intention in recommending the Decisions
Coaching was to help him understand and break this destructive pattern. Talk
about rebellious; he wanted nothing to do with me, or any *silly programs*. He
knew how to get a grip on his own life! Working Hank through the Decision
process, it was easy to see the two year old who hadn't grown beyond the temper tantrum stage and was in desperate need of a time out for reflection.

> **Transformation**
>
> *AFFIRMATION: I am joyously
> centered and safe as wonderful
> changes occur around me!*
>
> *Positive changes are coming.
> Old structures, beliefs, and ideas are
> falling away and will be replaced with
> vitality and new pathways.
> Soon you'll be seeing the world
> in a fresh way.*

Slowly we walked, slowly he grew, and as he grew he blossomed. There
were many tears, and many stories to unfold and a great deal of laughter. Hank was able to complete the program, recognize and understand
his destructive circles and realize that this was his opportunity to adopt new
decisions and stop the bad-decision-
get-caught-do-time-in-prison circle he had established. Hank became my first
Decisions star, he was released from his parole, got a job in a small company that
was on the brink of growth, secured a responsible position, soon purchased a small
row house and fully remodeled it. He turned his destructive decision cycle around.
He went on to meet a woman with two daughters; Hank was also able to teach
the girls the Decisions program, at a time when they were teenagers, vulnerable
to negative life choices.

How Are Decisions Circles Established?
Many of us have been raised in a world of over-indulgence. We fill our homes with

an over-abundance of stuff, and it becomes natural to provide plenty of toys, way beyond the few items that would nurture children's ease of selection and let their cognitive growth blossom. Parents and indulgent grandparents quickly provide every toy imaginable that becomes a mountain of molded plastic stuff which overflows in the rooms of most families with toddlers. The decision as to which item to play with, which one is demanding attention for the child, is over-whelming for their yet undeveloped cognitive brain and easily results in a tantrum of sheer frustration. Had they been given just two choices of toys at a time, their adult decision making skills would be stronger and more fulfilling than they are today.

Consider how the story plays out: you're two years old overwhelmed by the mountain of molded plastic in front of you, so you throw your toys all over the living room. Mom comes in and tells you to pick them up; overwhelmed you throw yourself on the floor and throw a temper tantrum, with no idea where or how to begin. This gets mom angry, so she gives you a gentle whack on the bottom. You continue to cry and carry on, but don't pick up the toys. Mom gives you a time out. After ten or fifteen minutes, you call Mom and say you'll pick up your toys. The next day and the next day and the next day – the same circle continues. As you get older, the circle changes with your age group, till you find Mom has been replaced with your teacher, boss or mate! Not a pretty picture. Most of us learn to step out of those patterns, some don't; thus Decisions Coaching steps in to help you to recognize and break those life patterns and re-educate your cognitive brain!

Choices empower when kept simple – not six items for baby, toddler and child, simply two! It isn't until adulthood that we can accept multiple choices with ease. Don't you sometimes find yourself overwhelmed standing in the ice cream store with twenty or more flavors to choose from and a long line of people waiting for your decision so they can make theirs? When that basic wiring has a strong and positive foundation, the baby/toddler/child/teen/adult can build on it and grow easily through all of their life stages. This foundation enables you to make sense and meaning out of making decisions and appropriately continue that process through adulthood. Decision patterns are built on prior cognitive memories, and appropriate decision making skills result in positive self-esteem.

Most of the people I work with have missed or did not have full advantage of these early learning and brain molding experiences. Although re-wiring your brain as an adult can be more challenging and effort-filled, it can be successfully accomplished.

There have been many stars in my Decisions practice; actually each individual with whom I've had an opportunity to work is a star – watching them grow has been my honor. One other client story provides a great look at decision downs, ups, downs and steady ups. Alice was the youngest child, unexpected by parents that were looking forward to being done with the restrictions of raising children. She was a cute and cuddly baby, and with older siblings still at home, she received all the early attention and learning experience that a baby needs. However, as she grew into her teens, the siblings had left home and her parents were ready to travel, often leaving her alone. When she graduated from high school, she was more than ready to get out on her own and *knew* she could take care of herself. As Alice began her climb up the ladder in the restaurant business, it seemed only natural for her to find a partner in the industry and together they had soon created a thriving upper class steak house. When disaster struck it was not of her doing, but it had a direct impact on her life. The business collapsed and the surrounding negative press in a small town lost Alice any opportunity to find another position. She was again alone in a world in which she was not able to cope.

Although she had been showered with early childhood attention, her adolescent decision skills never had the opportunity to mature. So it was not surprising that her world collapsed from over ambitious and immature choices. This time she would begin to rebuild with a young daughter and a new baby girl. She left the children with her grandmother, who was thrilled to have them, and moved to a new town for a fresh beginning.

I met Alice nearly twenty years ago. She was intensely focused on wanting to set a new foundation of understanding of how to not fall into the same destructive patterns. Unlike Hank, Alice immediately saw and understood her destructive circles and wanted to recognize more positive cognitive choices. She whizzed through the Decisions program, willingly completing her homework with clarity and determination. Her long term goal was a job in corporate America. She clearly understood she would be starting at rock bottom and that there would be a long climb. She challenged herself with positive goals, including re-uniting her family, which she was soon able to accomplish. Understanding how important higher education would be in her new goals, she took classes toward a business degree. As Alice reached each milestone, she continued to move ahead, taking every opportunity to advance her career.

Alice made the Decision to set her career goal at earning $100,000 a year. Through hard work, never turning back to her old habits and continuing to incorporate new decision patterns into her life every single day, she reached that goal several years ago. Alice had re-married and last year the couple decided that since Alice had reached her financial career goals, and her husband's career could easily provide all the family's needs, it was time for her stop that grueling climb. She realized she was happy to leave corporate America and was ready to start a home business so she could be more present in their young son's life. It continues to be an honor to watch Alice expand in her life and lift all who come within her circle to grow through her "I can do it!" example.

The years passed and although I had continued up-grading my coaching training, Denise's Soul Coaching, 28 Day Program really felt like it would be a perfect blend to enhance my Decisions coaching. I became a member of the Soul Coaching Certification training program, in the ninth class! What a moving and power-filled experience.

Soul Coaching is a life changing program. It is intensely transformative when completed with a facilitator to *coach* and encourage your progress. As you move through the dynamics as relating to Air *(mental)*, Water *(emotional)* Fire *(spiritual)* and Earth *(physical)* you discover the intimate workings of body, mind, heart and soul. You explore how each separate segment needs to operate smoothly for the whole to come together, to enable you to grow and succeed as a healthy individual, rather than being scattered, disorganized and cluttered. The program gently guides you to bring yourself into center, where you are given the opportunity to remain and grow.

Incorporating the Soul Coaching lessons into my clients' Decisions sessions, I am now able to help them at the roots of their Decision blockages, through the identification of the elements that have become their stumbling blocks. I gently guide clients back to the cognitive relearning tools that will reframe their life path and personal growth.

Prior to a client beginning their journey with me, I provide a packet of information for them to prepare. At our first visit we review this packet, which helps the client and me determine where the Decision Circle and Soul Blockage is located:

- *Air* ~ concentrating on *Mental* Clearing. Working with the energy of the client analyzing the source of their Decision circle, we discover how to re-pattern that habit. We look at the source from above and generally through journey, explore source and solution.

- *Water* ~ revealing that the Decision circle has an *Emotional* root. This is generally set in motion in early childhood (that two year old temper tantrum). Healing lifelong destructive circles is so freeing and life enhancing!

- *Fire* ~ looking at the *Spiritual* basis for Decision circles can be a challenging experience. Spirit, the fire that burns deep inside, is tricky. As with any fire, it can be explosive at unpredictable times. The expansion of inner being that comes in controlling Spirit-based Decision circles is delicate to explore, but like all other elements, rewarding when brought into balance with the whole.

- *Earth* ~ the *Physical* roots of our circles have aspects entangled deep within our being. The client generally finds that Earth roots may be revealed in struggles within the family of origin, often manifesting in seeking attention, positive or negative. Physical roots require a thorough detox of old instincts through an honest and open journey into family relations.

By providing many life enriching projects for my clients to develop their cognitive skills for clear decision making, they have the opportunity to grow from the source of their negative decision cycles. They learn to balance the elemental *Mental, Emotional, Spiritual* and *Physical* roots of their inner clutter, which manifests in outer decision clutter. Many of these projects grew out of my Soul Coaching training. At the first session, each client is given a homework assignment to create a Vision Board. A Vision Board provides insights to your inner soul, revealing truths that we often can't verbalize. Denise notes "The soul loves the truth," and on a soul level we know all things are possible. The work put into your Vision Board is a constant beacon, calling your *desires* into manifestation. It is an amazing experience to cut words and pictures from a magazine, paste them on a board, step back and look at your creation, and discover how many goals and higher intentions have come to light.

Decisions are the commitments that we make on a soul level that reveal our Spiritual Truths. When those Spiritual Truths are in-appropriate and/or destructive to you, everything in your life gets cluttered. Recognizing and being open to breaking or un-cluttering these destructive circles opens doors to new opportunities. Like that statement *Opportunity Knocking* – committing to exploring and disbanding destructive decision circles and empowering new positive Soul Practices, opens incredible doors!

Although we begin our journey with the identified root of the client's block, we travel through each element, cleaning and clearing the inner clutter and blockages as we go. The journey is rich in revelations and lifestyle rewards. Through incorporating the attributes of the Elements, the client goes back to that early brain building process, explores and incorporates the missing sensory pieces that were lacking in the cognitive brain-wiring at the time of infancy. This process enables the alignment of inner spiritual life and incorporates it into the outer decision-making world of reality. As a client's coach/mentor, I sit on the sideline and encourage, much like a basketball or football coach. My goal is to observe and mentor the client into change and maturity with a new understanding, an exciting set of tools and cognitive brain-rewiring that enable their Decision Skills to process faster and richer. By providing everyday life expanding cognitive exercises and empowering the client to continue growing in emotional maturity with each session, the skills continue to build and mature, now planted for life.

Along The Way . . .
Not long after I completed Soul Coaching Certification, my husband and partner of then nearly thirty years decided he wanted a divorce. Although we had been in counseling, trying to develop new cognitive skills for our own Decision process, this announcement came as a total surprise. We had relocated to Colorado several years before and I had nearly totally closed my Decisions Coaching practice. The decision had been to both retire in our new home state and enjoy a quieter, simpler life. Although he also announced he would file the paperwork, when that had still not happened by the end of the second year, a friend practically carried me into an attorney's office and wrote a check for his deposit. A year later, a judge handed down his decision; the divorce was final! I was not given any of the joint marital

financial assets (that's correct *NONE*), I would receive a small alimony check for seven years, although it was acknowledged that my now *ex* had the capacity and youth to earn much more money than I, he was fourteen years my junior.

Still wondering what my future would look like, I was rapidly approaching those serious senior years, with the ground under me rather muddy. I took three weeks for private hibernation and decision time. During that hiatus, positive get-up-and-go Decisions were made, that magical twinkle and the smile and dance began to return to my life. I was ready to re-climb the ladder-of-success one rung at a time, with a big smile on my face, radiating happiness from every pore of my body! The darkness now over, I faced the light and created new decisions. Furthermore during that hibernation time, I formulated an even more positive and power-filled plan to incorporate Soul and Decision coaching, to provide even greater benefit for clients. Six months later, it is wonderfully rewarding to watch my practice and opportunities flourish. Not only do I now work with individuals coaching one-on-one, I have also developed an exciting schedule of retreats for Women only, Men only, and Couples. We look at how Decisions impact our lives each and every day, and go directly to the *soul* of the issues.

As a member of the holistic community dedicated to enriching the lives of others through expanding personal growth experiences, I proudly witness each client as they move into their starring role in the new life they have chosen for them self. Having honed new and more positive cognitive skills and memories, each client moves forward with a new confidence and understanding of who they are. The maturity gained propels each and every client into a new role as they continue to expand their skills, able to stand proud, making sense and meaning out of their Decisions, through their new tools and lifestyle patterns.

The other day the phone rang, it was Alice. Although we had emailed now and again, we hadn't been in verbal contact for five years. We laughed, remembered, filled in the empty spaces, laughed and giggled some more. How proud we both are of each other and how we honor the change we have enabled in each other's lives! I told her that she was one of the stars of my chapter in an amazing book, and promised I would sign the first copy to her and fly her to a book signing! She challenged me to reach the same goal she reached . . . $100,000 a year. With the personal and professional Cognitive Decisions I have made and with the inner and outer Soul Clutter that has been cleared from my life, I believe that will happen.

The opportunity for change is there for each and every one of us. Come join the adventure and begin to develop your new positive cognitive toolbox, clear your Soul Clutter and sing! Be willing to wake up each and every morning laughing. Feel gratitude fill your heart and keep that twinkle in your eye. Giggles will lie simmering beneath the surface as people wonder what secret you are harboring. The quick and easy response is: breathing in Decision *freedom*, and the discovery of the magick of your soul being alive! Isn't that an exciting opportunity? You can do it; the water is warm; jump in and be prepared to swim into a new life!

❧

CHERYL UMBERGER
Lebanon, Pennsylvania, USA

CHERYL UMBERGER'S CHILDHOOD environment in an evangelical Christian church inspired her life passion for spiritual exploration. She continues to research and develop ways to assist others in bringing personal satisfaction to their spiritual practice while promoting acceptance and understanding of preferences and differences.

For fifteen years she chose to earn a living in the mortgage industry as a loan originator and found gratification working with finances and collaborating with people to achieve their dream of home ownership. Upon the birth of her fourth child, Cheryl left the mortgage industry to manage the unique challenges presented by her growing family.

In 2007 Cheryl trained as a Soul Coach™ with Denise Linn. Using the basic ideas of Soul Coaching®, Cheryl developed her own business called Gentle Journeys. Gentle Journeys provides Cheryl with a unique opportunity for her own personal development by connecting and inspiring women through classes, articles and individual coaching sessions.

Cheryl has created Welcome to Womanhood ceremonies that celebrate menarche (a girl's first period) in an effort to encourage young girls toward a foundation of self-worth and personal power. She enjoys writing about motherhood and finding creative ways to honor life cycles.

You can learn more about Cheryl and Gentle Journeys on the web at www.GentleJourneySoulCoach.com

Guide to Thrive as a Modern Mother

CHERYL UMBERGER

Who you are is enough. —DENISE LINN

*I*f you were to write out the job description for a mother, you would find a document that has no adequate beginning and no sufficient end. The term *mother* is not just a title but also a journey that a woman undertakes, with no clear map for direction. Once on the journey there are remarkably few mothers who would turn back, but most need encouragement and a little spark along the way.

When I had my fourth child I didn't know that simply having four children was going to make me an expert at balance in the eyes of others. At pre-school, at middle school, at football games and even at social events women would tell me their stories expecting that I could empathize and advise on the pressures that were weighing on them. I also found that my Soul Coaching business had a large base of women struggling with themselves as they mothered their children and soon realized that my own challenges were drawing to me women that I could learn from.

I commiserated with their woes and laughed with them at their joys. Deep inside I felt a stirring and a certainty that in order for a mother to thrive as an individual, valuable person, there would need to be a *Thriving Guide*. Yoga classes, massages and book clubs only put a bandage on the disruptions that occur in the souls of mothers. Our bandages are temporary and diminish our ability to grasp the part of us that is authentic. I wished for a few simple ideas to tote around with me. I wanted ideas that I could utilize during those times when I was merely surviving and not joyously thriving. There could be no set formula for success, but there absolutely could be a set of tools for each of us to sort through when we needed them and even a few essential tools that we would use every day.

I gathered some of my own lessons, those that I learned from others and a few key ingredients from Denise Linn's Soul Coaching program to develop my *Guide to Thrive as a Modern Mother*. These are four little thriving tips that bring contentment and joy to days that seem heavy with requirements and duties. Feel free to copy them into your journal or personalize them into your own pocket survival guide.

Thriving Tip One: *Who You Are Is Enough*
This phrase was coined by Denise Linn and is a fundamental teaching of Soul Coaching. Whether you have an infant crying all night, a child with special needs, a toddler that darts from one thing to the next, a young child with temper tantrums, a defiant teenager or a a an adult child stumbling through life, you have moments of feeling inadequate each day. Though this phrase is so simple, it is uniquely powerful. I have observed when my clients who are mothers first repeat this phrase, tears well up in their eyes. To go past the daily grind of expectations and touch your soul gently with this phrase is like resting peacefully underneath a gorgeous tree on a sunny day. When we dissect this phrase further, and apply it specifically to motherhood we find a means of developing personal poise and grace even in the most daunting parenting moments.

A) *Who you are is enough* because the spirit of your child chose you.

Yes, it's true! If you can believe that when you lose a loved one their spirit watches over you from the Light, then you can also understand that the soul of your child watched you before he or she arrived. Your child chose you to be his caregiver, her stability, his confidant and her human guide. There was no expectation prior to his arrival that you would be perfect, but rather that you were the best match for his journey.

B) *Who you are is enough* because your daily duties are not who you are.

Your soul shines a light and participates in a connected vibration to all things. THAT is who you are and you are here simply to be a part of this beautiful cycle of life. You don't need to play ten games of *Candy Land* each day, become more patient in the face of childhood theatrics, be better at algebra, attend more basketball games, participate in all school activities or have a spotless house in order to be worthwhile. Your daily duties are temporary *necessities* for this part of your journey, but they have no bearing on your authentic self.

It isn't necessary to find twenty minutes of meditation time in order to adopt this mantra and to feel its impact. Repeat it to yourself often no matter where you are and what you're doing, until it feels as true and as comfortable as your own skin.

Thriving Tip Two: *Know what your values are*
When you become a mother there is an enormous amount of morality that is placed upon you and, as time goes on, it becomes difficult to differentiate the things that you value in life from societal expectations. When you get lost in the societal expectation, you're reporting to that fictional mother image in your mind, as well as to the fictional image that is created of a model child, rather than to the true, complex individuals that you and your child really are.

Some societal expectations of children, which become guideposts and tasks for a mother to commit to, range from breastfeeding one's child, making sure a child behaves well in public, insuring that your child achieves academic excellence, is brought up with a traditional religious background, or that you comply with a doctor's standard of healthcare that doesn't agree with your own. The list could go on and on. Neat clothing, tidy hair, clean fingernails, a quiet voice, cooperation and compliance are all part of the theme of what is to be achieved in a *good* child, and a mother too often berates herself when her child doesn't fit the standard. Consistently striving for the high bar that is set by others will deteriorate your self-esteem and your quality relationship with your child.

One of my own common pitfalls is that of making sure that my children perform well in school. Since we live in the United States, this is determined largely by the highest letter grade that they receive. Many times I reach the point of anger when one of them is not performing to my expectations and it takes some time for me to unwind and get back to what my own values are, rather than succumbing to the societal expectation.

Coming to terms with your values is another foundation of Soul Coaching. I encourage you to write down your current values. Concentrate specifically on your values in connection with your life as a mother. As you review your list, decide if your life is consistent with your values.

In my own personal example you can see that I value personal responsibility and accountability more than I do an *A* for my children. If I am scolding them merely because their grade point average does not meet what other parents would expect of them, I become miserable and my children would withdraw from me. When I focus on instilling in them that their school work is their personal responsibility and that they are accountable for completing it thoroughly and completely now, just as they will be for any work that they perform as a means of earning money later in life, I am behaving more authentically.

When I am in tune with my own values I have the best opportunity to pass them along to my children in a meaningful way. When I reduce myself to trying to achieve what others expect of me and what others expect of my child, I create a relationship with my child that is disharmonious.

Making a list of your values is a most effective way of determining what they are. You may want to create one list that includes your current values and a second list that includes the values that you would like to have in order to be more in line with your authentic self. Be gentle with yourself as you gradually release the expectations that have been placed on you, and replace them with your innermost desires communicated from your soul. I've included a limited itemization of values that will get your list started, but don't be afraid to be creative and include your own.

Values for Your Consideration

Learning	Intimacy	Loyalty	Resolution	Boldness
Intensity	Love	Freedom	Sensuality	Beauty
Mastery	Motivation	Neatness	Sincerity	Capability
Obedience	Optimism	Sacrifice	Closeness	Open-mindedness
Endurance	Appreciation	Balance	Benevolence	Adventure

Thriving Tip Three: *Eliminate "I've been so busy"*

At least once a day I hear this phrase from a mother. It may be a conversation that I overhear at the gym or the grocery store or simply during a phone call that I have with one of my friends. Sometimes, I hear it come from me as well and then I cringe. This simple little phrase has become so prevalent that it zaps the enthusiasm out of your day and deteriorates your ability to interact with others from the base of your authentic self.

In order to understand why this over-used phrase affects you negatively as a mother, we need to understand when and why the phrase is used.

As a mother your obligations to your children infringe upon the personal time that you have in a day. It is difficult to meet the needs of their schedules and also to allow time for the things that you like to do. The fact remains that how you choose to spend your time remains your own. When you use the "I've been so busy" phrase, you are not being honest with yourself about how you choose to spend your time.

> **Embracing**
>
> *AFFIRMATION: I embrace and love all of my life.*
>
> *Embrace all of your life, both the dark and the light. Dance with your shadow and reclaim parts of yourself that you've denied. Embrace your past and what has been hidden or denied.*

The reason that we use this phrase is because the excuse is comfortable and makes us feel like the other person involved in the conversation will continue to like us and not find us lacking. Unfortunately, everyone realizes that this is an excuse and it diminishes relationships and creates uncomfortable circumstances. You are not acting from a place of power when you use this excuse. When you say this to a friend, you are giving away your power and creating a situation where you will feel compelled to do something at a later time to make up for excusing yourself from a phone call, party, get together or activity.

When you are grounded in your most authentic self, you recognize that how you spend each precious moment is absolutely your choice. It doesn't excuse you from obligations such as driving your child to school or cooking dinner, rather it means that you approach each obligation as a choice and understand that the remaining parts of the day are in your hands as well.

Following is an example of practical application of this concept and ways to communicate to others in a manner that retains integrity on both sides of the conversation:

A close friend invites you to a girl's night out party in her home. The party is taking place on a Sunday evening, which is when you typically have time to spend reading a book. You know when you receive the invitation that, although it sounds fun, you don't want to attend the party. Your choices are:

- Go to the party to support your friend.

- Wait until the last minute to respond and tell your friend that you've been so busy that you forgot about the invitation and that it won't be possible for you to make it.

- Don't respond at all and when you next speak to your friend apologize profusely and say that you've been so busy that you completely forgot.

- Make up a story about having other plans, but refusing to name them.

Let's face it, we've all done this! None of those choices make us feel good and they don't make your friend feel good either. The excuse serves only to create guilt, which is a useless emotion that doesn't spur you on to being your best self.

An option here would be to be honest with yourself and your friend immediately upon receiving the invitation. Express honesty from your place of power and it will sound similar to: "I received your invitation for your party on Sunday night. Many of my other nights are filled with obligations for the kids, so on Sunday nights I choose to stay at home. I feel that this helps me to re-charge my batteries and spend time honoring myself. Thank you for thinking of me and inviting me and I'll wish you all a great time on that night!"

Being honest with your friend alleviates tension building up in the relationship. By being authentic and letting your friend know that you need time to yourself, you have eliminated any possibility that she will infer that there is something wrong in the relationship. It is powerful to make a choice and to be open about it. It is diminishing to both the person receiving your excuse and to yourself when you make them.

Mothering absolutely requires skillful use of time. When you start to tell others and yourself that you are so busy that you can't call a friend, exercise, take a class, write a book or take action on any desire that you have, your mind will begin to believe it. Once you're caught in the trap, you increase the possibility of depression and frustration creeping into your life.

This simple conversational phrase works to convince us that outside forces create our circumstances and dictate our days. Do not relinquish the power to be honest with others and with yourself about how you spend your time. You may truly want to spend time catching up with a friend on the phone, but creating the time to do that may feel like an overwhelming task, so you resign yourself to the fact that life is too busy.

Giving in to that thinking provides too much opportunity for wallowing to begin, and for discontent to get a foothold in your life. Be gentle with yourself and take baby steps, but each time you either tell yourself that you are too busy to do something that you would like to do, or you make the excuse to someone else, stop and find a way for more honest expression.

Unexpected opportunities may arise when you shift your thinking and your conversations. I had been thinking about renewing my certification to teach fitness classes, but every time the thought arose I defeated it by telling myself that I wouldn't have time to teach a class because my toddlers have demands during the day and my adolescent children have activities in the evenings. As a result, I avoided the director of fitness at the gym for many months. Each time she asked me about being ready to teach classes, I blew off the conversation with my *too busy* excuse.

One day, after taking her class I finally spoke to her and expressed my precise concerns. I told her that my youngest would wind up in the childcare center for more than the maximum one hour if I taught a class and I had nowhere else to bring him for care. I explained that I would not be available for evening classes and that I knew that I could not commit to the studying it would take to pass the test for certification renewal.

To my surprise she explained that the policy of the facility allows childcare for two hours and that it wouldn't be necessary for me to update my certification. Within this particular organization it was acceptable for an instructor to meet only their internal standards. By using my *too busy* excuse I had spent months squirming away from something that I would have really liked to do. Had I been up front right from the beginning I would have learned that this opportunity was available to me on terms that definitely met my needs.

Thriving Tip Four: *Remember the Good, Dark Mother*
Your most authentic self exists in polarity just like all other things in our universe. There is no ideal mother. There are only human mothers with an enormous capacity for love, gentleness, patience, wisdom, compassion and kindness. Those are the qualities that we label *good* and for every one of them, within each mother exists the opposite capacity for impatience, volatility, boredom, frustration, depression and inadequacy. We label these qualities as *bad*.

Mothers are more apt to mentally flog themselves, analyze their behavior and criticize their own actions more than any other group of people I have met. The responsibilities of the job are not set up for a woman to feel successful and fulfilled. After all, children themselves with their limited ability for expression will declare that you are a *bad* mother, that they don't like you anymore or announce that you are *unfair*. The reward system for the job of mothering only exists within oneself, unlike other employment where you may receive bonuses or recognition for a job well done.

Trying to identify with only what you determine as *good* will undermine your health and your effectiveness as a mother. Being present with your child and acknowledging your limitations allows her to accept the humanity within herself.

Again, honesty and honoring your authentic self plays an important role. On a day when your patience is short, make sure that you communicate that to your child so he is aware that you are likely to respond unfavorably to his demands. If you have a young child that is not able to understand your predicament, make sure that your spouse and your extended support system is aware that you're having a difficult day.

Once you do that, if someone is able to give you some time to yourself, honor the way that you feel. Spend the day in bed; take a walk; dance out your feelings and move into them without labeling yourself as *bad* or your feelings as *dark*. Giving them room to exist allows them expression and increases the speed at which the dark mood will pass.

If you have no support system and your child has only that impatient, uptight YOU to exist with on that particular day, choose to set aside anything that is not a true requirement of you. Don't do the dishes or the laundry, take a sick day from work, order out for food or do whatever is necessary to eliminate pressure. Accepting that part of yourself that can't measure up to your ideals is necessary. When you accept your limitations, you will not beat yourself up for shortcomings, and space is created for flourishing when you have the energy to do so.

A day cannot exist without dark and light and so a mother does not thrive without accepting that both exist within her.

There are no greater emotions experienced or shared in the world than those of a mother, but it is a mistake to believe that each woman can carry these huge responsibilities without a breakdown of courage from time to time. It is a rare woman who makes this journey with ease. Women are continually bombarded with media images as well as the ideologies of their youth, which together create a fictional, *ideal mother* that exists in the mind.

Whether you've arrived at the door of motherhood accidentally, by adoption, with fertility assistance, as a step-mother or with careful planning, you probably arrived with expectations. Sadly, the expectations that we set for ourselves have their roots in this fictional image that we create and cling to in our minds. This results in a mothering journey that is clouded by feelings of defeat, a depletion of self-confidence, strong feelings of inadequacy and continual self-doubt.

The authentic self of most modern mothers lies buried beneath this image of an *ideal mother*. In order to identify your most authentic self, and for this authentic self to be present for the children in your life, it is vital to dismantle this false image. There is vivaciousness that exists in our soul, and without fail our instincts are guiding us to listen. By tapping into the wisdom of our soul, our authenticity becomes defined, and the way is clear for us to live our most meaningful, mothering life.

∾

ULRIKE BEHRE-BRANDES
Gelsenkirchen, Germany

Ulrike Behre-Brandes lives a busy family life in Gelsenkirchen, Germany. Meeting Denise Linn and attending her seminars since 1993 has been a turning point in her life. In August 2003 Ulrike Behre-Brandes was personally certified in Soul Coaching® by Denise Linn.

As a coach and a spiritual teacher her goal is to inspire people to find their own inspiration, their own expression and to find a place of creativity within themselves. She holds a safe space for her clients, to make it easier for them to connect with who they really are. This is what makes her heart sing!

Her background includes energy work with Sion R. Windelov, movement work with Gabrielle Roth (5 Rhythms®), training in meditation with Petra Schneider and traveling worldwide studying people and cultures.

She runs seminars, workshops and holds lectures on different topics. She is also involved with primary education. Contact Ulrike at bebra50 @hotmail.com

For further information visit: www.SoulCoaching-BehreBrandes.de

Transitions

ULRIKE BEHRE-BRANDES

The Soul Coaching program can assist your menopause passage.
A fresh and renewed you is waiting!

"*I*s my menopause passage a transition?"
"Do you really think it is a spiritual journey?"
Many women have asked me these questions in the last few years. As a Soul Coach who works in Germany I have often assisted women to discover who they really are, so they can live a life which reflects the truth about themselves. There is something these women all have in common: they have been going through the transition of menopause. By working with the Soul Coaching *tools,* their passages have been made easier and more comfortable for them. They did not remain stuck during the process of transition. This is very important.

When it comes to menopause, most women focus on what they will lose, so they often feel negatively about it. But once they start working with the Soul Coaching tools, they discover how much they will gain, and this changes their whole outlook. They suddenly get new and inspiring ideas. That is what we all need in times of transition. We do not need such intensive forms of knowledge anymore. I think there is great advantage for many of us as women and as Soul Coaches to look at the Soul Coaching tools as simple and inspiring methods to make a menopause passage comfortable and light-filled in fresh new ways.

To all the women who have not yet experienced menopause – don't think of it as a loud *bang*. It is more like a series of small, subtle changes – concerning your emotional balance, the way you feel your body, the way you conduct your daily routine. There are lots of books which describe the physical reactions of the body caused by hormonal imbalance, like hot flashes, sweats during the night, sleeplessness etc. When you read about these possible body reactions don't panic! Take a deep breath, relax and try to remember your puberty. Your body has made it through puberty and it will make it through menopause – no matter what! But let me tell you one very important fact. Every body, and this includes your body, too, will react differently. No matter what your individual reaction might be, it is time to get deeply and fully connected to your body. What is the best way to connect with your physical body? It is to love and to honor it!

This is not so easy for many of us. Women have been trained to look at their bodies in a very critical way. But being critical will separate us even more from our bodies. We trust others more than ourselves. We give away authority and forget that our bodies never lie to us. When you love your body unconditionally, you can listen to it. Be patient, compassionate and listen! *If there is something I should know, what would it be?* This has been my favorite question when I've talked to every part of my body during my yoga stretches in the morning. And on one particular day an answer came so simply and clearly. It was about taking a rest. My whole system needed a rest. I have been so caught up in the activities of my life that I had forgotten about taking a rest. I had simply forgotten about the importance of stillness and regeneration.

What came to my mind was: "Take a sabbatical year!" At the same moment a flush of joy, a wave of energy filled my whole body! 2003 was to be my first sabbatical and in 2008 another one followed. Taking a sabbatical year may not be the right formula for you because there are no right recipes. But maybe this will inspire you to find out what will work for you. Is it a weekend of regeneration once a month, or a day of stillness every week? It is up to you to find out!

During my time of regeneration I spent lots of time in nature – feeling the cool wind on my face, the fresh water on my feet and the warm sun on my skin – that reminded me of my childhood. In our busy adult life we forget about the elements of nature: air, water, fire, earth, and the healing forces which they offer to us. Lying in the grass feeling the earth under my body, smelling the sweetness of the flowers around me. . . This connects me with Mother Earth and gives me the chance to be still and receptive. *I too am a part of the rhythms of nature, and everything is perfect just the way it is. There is nothing to do, just be. Who I am is enough.* My sudden inspiration opened many new doorways for me. That same year, 2003, I became a certified Soul Coach. Denise Linn's words: *The soul loves the truth,* have echoed deeply inside me since then.

When I run a menopause workshop I start with what Denise Linn calls Earth Week. It is about getting into contact with your body. The participants feel inspired by all the wonderful choices they have with the daily Soul Coaching assignments on different levels.

Here is a sample of assignments which are often chosen from the Soul Coaching program:

- Make a commitment that empowers the body.
- Take action to detoxify the body.
- Plan rejuvenation times.
- Awakening natural rhythms within you.
- Bring nature into your home.
- Create a place in your home for your soul.

"Locate one place in your home that will be your power spot with objects that inspire you. Use this place for meditation and relaxation, a place to renew your energy," Denise Linn advises. When you are doing Soul Coaching by yourself, I suggest listening to the short Soul Journeys Denise has created on Hay House Radio. Just look into the show archives to find the right ones. In my seminars I often use Denise Linn's CD: *Secrets and Mysteries. The Glory and Pleasure of being a Woman.*

Some of us may feel overwhelmed by the choices we have to make concerning the daily assignments and affirmations. When this happens I offer a very easy exercise to keep the energy flowing. I call it *Body Language.* Listen to any music you like and let your body move to it. Don't judge your movements! You are not on a dance floor. Let your body move the way it wants to. There is no right or wrong, only movement. Do it twenty minutes a day, or do it for as long as it feels good for you. By doing this, you will start being receptive to your body language. There may be days when your movements will be flowing and receptive. On other days you might create a wild dance, stamping your feet on the ground, feeling Mother Earth when shaking your body. And there are times when you dance abruptly with short hard body movements. Of course there will be the soft meditative dance, too. Doing this as a daily routine, you will be surprised how easy it is to forget the dancer and just be the dance. In this situation your body becomes a kind of melting pot for your thoughts and emotions; you will feel it as a vessel for your soul, because suddenly there is now space open for your soul. When you go beyond the control of your mind you become connected with the truth of your soul. Your soul loves the truth!

It might be that you are suddenly aware of some old patterns which are coming up to the surface. These may be old judgments about yourself . . . *I am not good enough . . . I can't do this because . . .* etc. You should know this: Your mind thrives on judgment! Judgments are a very controlling energy. Don't identify with your thoughts and belief systems. You are not your thoughts; you are not your mind. You are a soul in a physical body on a spiritual journey. Absolute acceptance is important: It is as it is. Breathe in *self acceptance*, breathe out *self judgment*! By doing this you become free in any particular situation; you are free from the control of your mind. You are in the present moment. This is important because your mind always wants to take you somewhere else.

This brings us to the middle of Air Week, which is about clearing your mental self. To discover your authentic self, be honest in your self-appraisal. In the daily Soul Coaching exercises you will find a lot of inspiration about how to let go of old patterns that no longer serve you. Where are you in your life? Where would you like to be? Be honest with yourself and notice the areas in your life where the distance is great.

What my clients love doing during Air Week is the daily assignment of clutter clearing, along with the affirmation that is appropriate to it. In times of transition it is helpful to reorganize your environment. I have had clients who live in houses or flats where nothing has changed for the last twenty years. Although their children have grown up and gone away to university, you can still find their rooms intact. There is this *empty nest* syndrome and it has not yet been filled.

Whenever you feel a stagnant energy around you, clutter clearing in your environment has a corresponding effect on the mental clutter inside you. This effect can be very powerful as it opens a space for new ideas and clarity to come in. The action of clutter clearing gives your mind the impression of being in control. This helps you to stay focused. The more clutter clearing you do, the more you will discover a dynamic clarity which comes into your life. This is very important in times of transition.

To get more clarity about the direction of your life, ask yourself: Why am I here?

Denise Linn has said "Often the way that our soul talks to us is through synchronicities, coincidences and signs." So take time to listen carefully. Some of my clients use the *Soul Coaching Oracle Cards* by Denise Linn to get an idea of what their soul mission could be. So find out what will work for you. Denise tells us that "when you write your mission statement or say it out loud, you should get an immediate rush of energy, strength and vitality because the words resonate with your soul." All I can say is that my mission statement gave me the courage and strength to write this chapter for this book.

Water Week is about clearing and cleansing the emotional self. To detoxify your body you can increase the daily amount of water you drink. By telling the truth about what you feel, it is easier for you to find inner peace. For women going through menopause, there can be a pitfall in this emotional territory. Major chemical changes in the body can cause feelings that are mainly related to those chemical changes. So there is a danger of getting lost or being overwhelmed by those feelings without knowing that they are simply a result of hormonal changes. The best you can do is to become the secret observer of your feelings. It is similar to puberty but you are wiser now. So don't let your emotions control you; don't let the hot flashes control you! Don't identify with them. It's simply a hot flash, nothing else, because your hormonal system is trying to find a new balance.

You are not your emotions; they are just an energy – you can step out of your drama any time you want to. By doing this; you open up a space for fresh inspiration to come in. Maybe you will get a new idea about what will work best for you in dealing with the physical symptoms of your transition. For example, you might get a nudge to try acupuncture treatments, or herbal remedies etc. Find out which treatment resonates with you!

To strengthen your life force it is important to find out what is uplifting your energy and what brings your energy down. Make a list. In times of transitions it is more than important to avoid particular situations or a particular person who reduces your energy. If you can't avoid a person or a situation that lowers your energy, keep yourself clear. You don't need to carry someone else's burden, not of your family etc. It is too much weight during your menopause passage. Make an inner statement: I will not take part in your game. I release all burdens! By doing this you can reprogram an old pattern. Don't say *yes* when you mean *no*! Don't try to please everyone! You are not everybody's darling! Try to increase your *juicers* instead, persons and situations that keep your energy uplifted.

Each one of us has a life story, a personal history. But many of us are not happy with it and feel resistance. We feel that something should happen that has not happened yet. Many of us are not friends with life. Somehow we always seem to feel a lack of something and everybody else is responsible for it. This makes us feel like victims. But we are not our stories; we are not our feelings! We are so much more. We are a soul on a spiritual journey and we can make choices.

If you feel there is a blockage in your life, be aware of the feeling. Get in touch with it, feel it, accept it, act it out, give love to the situation, let it go and give thanks! For some of us this can be very scary. But you don't have to do this all by yourself! You can always ask for spiritual guidance. Maybe you will look for a certified Soul Coach to assist you. A Soul Coach doesn't judge, because we are all One, just different aspects of the divine energy. He or she will hold a safe space for you. In this space you can receive things more easily; the knowing can flow better and you can connect with who you really are.

I also suggest seeking the assistance of a Soul Coach when you are dealing with relationship and childhood issues. There may be old wounds coming up to the surface that wish to be healed. Every child wants to be accepted, to be loved just the way he or she is. When

> ### Power
>
> *AFFIRMATION: I am a radiant, glorious, powerful being!*
>
> *Express your strength with grace, and take back your power. It's safe to own your gifts. Accept that within you is a place of divine strength and inner ability.*

you get in touch with feelings of *not being good enough*, of *being ashamed of something* etc., take a deep breath and be aware of the feeling! Awareness is the key to stepping out of your drama; it connects you with the present moment. In the present moment you will realize that it is just a feeling, a sort of energy, nothing else. Indeed it takes practice to let go, not to get attached to your feelings! The more you practice, the more you can catch yourself a little bit earlier. A certified Soul Coach is perfect to assist you during this process. It is the safe space that helps you to dissolve limitations and blockages and go beyond them to be free.

Connecting with the child you once were is useful for you in many ways. It helps you to get in touch with the dreams you once had, to get connected with the joy, the courage, the innocence and the playfulness. Acknowledging this part of yourself will rejuvenate your whole being. It will strengthen your life force. There is something magical about it, and beyond this you are not so serious about everything. Your mind will not understand it but will accept it! After dealing with so much emotional stuff, this is the time when many of us feel peace within ourselves. We consciously choose our lives but we are not our lives. We are so much more! We feel a deep gratitude and feel connected to the Creator of all life.

This is a turning point in our menopause passage. From this point on, we get into our power and strength and we want to express the truth and honor of ourselves. For some of us a sudden pitfall can emerge. Some women can get in touch with an old fear-based program that is like: If I come into my power, my strength and my inner beauty, I will be judged. Something will happen to me. I am not safe to tell my truth, to show who I am.

These are very old programs. Especially here in Europe a lot of women were persecuted during the Inquisition and $15^{th}–18^{th}$ Century Witch hunts. It has been estimated by some that there were as many as three million women tortured and killed because of their knowledge of medicinal herbs, for assisting at childbirths etc. This is incredible! And there are still no accurate official figures about it. So if some of you get in touch with this energy field, with a feeling of being judged or not being safe – don't take it personally! Be aware of it, acknowledge it but don't get attached to it! Be reassured that it is safe for you to be here; trust and ask for guidance. Focus on your goals; focus on service and everything is going to work out fine.

If you want to give birth to new projects, new ideas or whatever you wish to create, you have to step out of your comfort zone and take risks. Sometimes this can be frightening. When I heard about this book, it made my heart sing and I wanted to engage in this project. But there was a challenge to face: I had to write in English. But English is not my native language; my native language is German! So I felt the fear: "Maybe I will fail." But I did it anyway. My fears are not who I am!

Your menopause passage is a time when you consciously acknowledge that you are the creator of your life, and your creations are unlimited. You can create a home that reflects who you are; you can create a job which is perfect for you, a sexual life that is fulfilling etc. Trust your intuition and follow your heart! You don't need to be perfect; leave space for the inspiration to come in, so spirit can guide you! What do you have to know to create a life that is fulfilling? Have fresh new ideas about it. Realize the power of your intentions, thoughts and feelings, and use Soul Coaching tools to manifest it in this world.

Look for a Soul Coach who holds Vision Board classes! Creating a Vision Board or an altar are wonderful tools to project your thoughts, dreams and desires into a conscious form. A Soul Coach assists you in finding powerful affirmations that will work for you and will create Soul Journeys and rituals that help you to stay focused. Your soul loves ceremonies and rituals. Trust the process and take action! That's what Fire Week is all about! Create – and new doorways will be open for you. All you need is within you.

By consciously choosing your menopause passage as a chance to get connected with your soul, you create your life in fresh new ways. This has an effect on your whole being; it renews your energy on a whole new level. Be aware of this: Wisdom is not always written in words. It is within the energy of the transformation, and beyond the transformation, in the energy of *being*. Simply *be*, in absolute acceptance of the being you are. When you choose: *I am going to be who I am. I want to express that. I want to celebrate it!* you will radiate an energy that affects and helps everybody around you to be who they are. This is a great service to the world. But don't live your life too seriously. Laugh; have fun; embrace your life and be grateful for everything!

∽

Bibliography

Linn, Denise. *Soul Coaching.* Hay House, 2003.
Linn, Denise. *Soul Coaching Oracle Cards.* Hay House, 2005.
Linn, Denise. *Secrets & Mysteries.* Hay House, 2002.
Roth, Gabrielle. *Sweat Your Prayers.* Tarcher/Putnam New York, 1997.

Audios

Linn, Denise. *Secrets & Mysteries.* QED Recording Services Ltd.
Linn, Denise. *Phoenix Rising.* QED Recording Services Ltd.
Linn, Denise. *Soul Coaching.* Hay House Radio, Show Archives.

BERTE WINDING-SØRENSEN
Norway

BERTE ALWAYS THOUGHT she'd get herself a proper education. Instead she's been educated by life, as all her attempts at studying were thwarted by her health. She has tried several courses of study; over time she studied science, orthopaedic engineering, and product design. She's had a diverse work experience having worked as a fork lift driver and foreman at the port, as a silk screen printer, and a sales assistant in both hardware and designer goods – all while trying to understand her health and why she experienced what she did; trying to make sense of life. Her life has been her laboratory as she's tried and tested numerous therapies; some that helped, some that didn't.

She has lived in the greater Oslo area most of her life, and now lives in a small town with her husband, their two children and a cat. Berte continuously works to carve out her spot while caring for those she loves.

Being the daughter of two scientists she finds that seeking new knowledge is in her blood, as well as a wish to share it with others. She has come to the conclusion that she needs to take her life and its joys and challenges as a spiritual exercise, and is happy to share her experiences and to guide others in accepting their own.

Contact Berte at www.WindingPathCoaching.com

Living a Better Life with MS

BERTE WINDING-SØRENSEN

Maybe now I'd be able to hear what my soul was trying to whisper to me.

On 31 October 1994 I got a diagnosis I never imagined possible. I'd had various symptoms all through my life (like strange pains that came and went, fatigue, vertigo and dizziness), but surely it was something easily curable? My test results had returned and my physician looked at me with pity, sighed and said, "Well, you've got the right to know what it says," and went on to tell me I had *Multiple Sclerosis.*

My mind was reeling. The numbness in my legs surely was just a slipped disk? Unfortunately not. Two days before this my dad had died in a car crash and because of that I knew that I'd lose the child I carried at the time. Mother Nature is wise; I did indeed lose the child, which eventually was OK with me; I had trouble enough digesting my diagnosis and the loss of my dad, whom I'd been very close with. It took a few months before I was able to cope, but finally I started to get a grip on my situation.

In early summer '95 my dream came true: After three days of tests I was accepted as a student at what's now the Department of Industrial Design at Oslo School of Architecture and Design, and in August I started my studies. I had dropped out of studies before, because my health had crashed, but figured that now, when I knew what was the matter, I'd do brilliantly. Two details had slipped my mind – 1) That this is a very stressful course of study, and 2) It's not enough to know what the problem is, you need to act accordingly. Having a disease that makes you literally allergic to stress is not a good combination with a stressful program, and in March '96 I ended up in hospital, with complete loss of eyesight on one eye. The eyesight eventually returned, but never got back to the same level as before.

Late in that year I was in New York, and looked at all the health related alternative books in one of the many big bookstores that city is blessed with. So many! I figured I'd try something I'd never done before, so I closed my eyes and said to myself "Go to the book that will help me the most." I imagined I'd feel a big hand leading me to the right book, but that didn't happen. I just went over to the bookshelves, bent down, and picked up *Anatomy of The Spirit*, by Caroline Myss. The book overlaps the seven Christian sacraments with the seven Hindu chakras and the seven levels of the Kabbalah's Tree of Life to create a map of the human energy anatomy. I read through it once, and then in the spring next year I brought out a journal and worked my way through the book, thoroughly answering the questions for self examination. It was an excruciating process. I felt ashamed by some of the answers, but, most importantly, I learned to forgive, and I learned about blessings in disguise.

It wasn't easy being me, growing up. One thing was the tension that came from my dad's alcoholism, but worse was the incessant tormenting and bullying at school. I was constantly told that I was both ugly and stupid, which of course wasn't true – I know now I look reasonably good and I'm definitely not stupid, but I soon learned to hide my talents because being proud of my achievements meant being stomped on even harder.

Eventually I had the lowest self esteem possible, even though there was a resilient part of me that kept fighting and focused on the few, glorious exceptions where I'd got approval – and kept me afloat until I moved away and found anonymity in a larger city. I carried a lot of resentment towards several people, but finally, through the exercises in *Anatomy Of The Spirit*, I understood what this was doing to me and started pulling my energy back. I worked for weeks, forgiving and releasing my tormentors and bullies; everybody who'd done me wrong. It felt like a great weight was lifted off me. According to my mother, I was transformed.

Then I started receiving Cranio-Sacral Therapy treatments. They were amazing and lifted my functioning level up even further. My CS therapist is a wonderfully aware woman and through her gentle guidance I experienced regressions which healed me further, and when my husband and I tried the *The Journey* (developed by Brandon Bays) technique at home in 2003 and it had stopped at a feeling in my chest several times, she held the area while I went back in to take a look. That experience blew my mind.

I closed my eyes and imagined going down some stairs to my chest area and opening the door. "Oh," I said out loud, "It's a galaxy!" I saw a gently swirling spiral of light, like a spiral galaxy with the brightest stars imaginable. "I carry a galaxy in my chest!" Immediately I was filled with a love so big, so strong, my tears started flowing and I heard a voice saying "Finally, my girl, finally you saw it," and I knew I was talking to the Creator, the Goddess. In my mind I just sat there next to her, soaking up her love, but eventually she said "You need to go now. You've got work to do. You can't stay." I got up and left and walked straight into a big fat beam of light that filled my every pore, bursting out of every part of me. Simultaneously my therapist rapidly drew her breath, so I realized she'd also noticed something. When I asked her afterwards, she said I'd suddenly been filled with the strongest, purest energy she'd ever felt. And me? I was floating. Even though I felt thoroughly healed by this energy, unfortunately my symptoms didn't disappear.

In October 1998 we were blessed with a beautiful daughter, and a son in April 2001. I nursed religiously, because I had read somewhere that among people diagnosed with MS, more had been bottle fed than among the population in general (and I was one of them), but in 2004 I felt I had done my duty and weaned my son. I was ready for my first week alone, without kids or husband, since my babies were born.

In May I went to New York to visit my cousin who lived in Manhattan. I love NYC and really looked forward to spending some time with her since we always have a great time together. She had a surprise for me, though. A session with the psychic Tony Le Roy. "When you come, I just know you would learn a lot by having a consultation with this great psychic," my cousin told me. "He's really cool and gives you all sorts of information." Whoa! Wait a sec – a psychic? I had no problem with people being psychic, but wasn't sure I was ready to meet one myself. My curiosity won and besides, hadn't I decided to be open to the serendipitous coincidences in life? This would be a new, grand experience. "You'll love him!" my cousin said. I was more cautious.

Well, I needn't have been, because it was a great experience. Among other things, he told me I had to choose. I had to make a choice about what to do. Oh, the curse of being multitalented – I had no idea what to choose. "It won't be set in stone, you know," he said. "You can always change to something else later, but you need to choose." That he also said *I'd become a coach* didn't register at all – I had no idea what a coach was. I only noticed this after replaying my tape from the session.

Back home I began looking into things I loved – could any of these be a possible occupation for me? Because of my MS, I'd been on disability since '96, and while it removed a lot of ill health inducing stress, it was also rather boring. I meditated. I started drawing mandalas. I got interested in symbols and their meanings. This led to searching the Internet for books on symbols.

One of the several I bought was *SIGNPOSTS – How to Interpret the Coincidences and Symbols in your Life*, by Denise Linn. I loved it, it tickled something deep inside, so I went back to the bookstore and ordered eight more books by Denise, one of them was *Soul Coaching – 28 days to Discover Your Authentic Self*. How promising! Maybe now I'd be able to find out what to do with my life. The book arrived and I dived right in – and decided I needed a course. This was just what I was looking for! Maybe now I'd be able to hear what my soul was trying to whisper to me. I was sure it was something, but I was unable to hear it. And so it was that in October '04 I was flying to the USA again, for my first trip ever to California.

The certification course was wonderful, if wet and cold (the weather surprised us all.) We were soaked; I ached all over from all the sitting, but I had some wonderful experiences. Some of the best came when we were practicing Soul Journeys on each other. Oh joy! I was One with all of Creation; the leaves on the trees were part of me, the grass, the seas, the stars. The wars and struggles around the globe made me sad (in a weird, accepting way), but there was so much love it took my breath away. Talk about high!

Back home it was time to go through the 28 Days to open myself to the wisdom of my soul, and a quote at the beginning of the course had already got my mind spinning – *What would you do if you absolutely knew you could not fail?* What, indeed? I mean, really? I'd heal myself for sure, but what then? Become an artist? Be a spaceship pilot? I wasn't sure at all.

The first day's affirmation got my inner self straightened out a bit – *My evaluation of myself is not who I am.* Oh, it's not? Then who am I? I noticed that my MS had become too big a part of my identity, and that had to change. Because, primarily I'm me. Not *MS*, not *MSme* or *meMS*, but me. And even though there are several books describing the connections between thought patterns and diseases, that doesn't mean that I'm a bad person even if I don't like the characteristics of my particular struggle.

Maybe it wasn't such a bad idea after all to take a look at these theories about how we manifest illness. I had already cottoned on to the idea that an auto-immune disease meant that deep down I didn't like myself very much – after all, what other reason would there be for attacking myself? This is a topic I've returned to time and again; trying to understand how I rather unknowingly had manifested this disease in my body. I didn't really want it, of course. Who wants a potentially severe, crippling disease after all? But I also had to admit that deep down I had wanted to become ill. Because I hated my life growing up. I had a hard time both at school, and outside. Just enough positive stuff to keep me going and stop me from giving up and ending it all, but not enough to make me thoroughly enjoy life.

And I'd discovered that if I were ill, I could stay at home and I got care – love and affection. That's not to say that I didn't get it if I went to school, but staying at home made *that* the major experience of my day, instead of harassment and belittling. So of course being ill was perceived as *good*. Somehow that had happened enough to lodge itself securely into my brain. So much so that even when my life changed and

Healing

AFFIRMATION: Phenomenal healing energy flows through every cell in my body!

Healing is occurring.
You're a natural healer.
You're on the mend, and/or the situation is being resolved.
Have faith that it's happening.

I started to feel good about it, when I found the most wonderful supportive and gorgeous man I later married, this notion didn't change. Because it had already started to build a disease; a disease it took me ages to get diagnosed.

Denise keeps repeating "the soul loves the truth" and there is a reason for that. A very simple one – it's true! It's also very necessary to hear. If you tell yourself that everything is fine when deep inside you know that it is not, your soul suffers. I'd told myself that I had a good handle on my MS, but did I really? I mean, really? I wasn't so sure anymore, and my soul soared at the thought. Interesting. It tickled me pink to think I'd been wrong, probably because it was a very good thing to discover it, so that I could get another push in the right direction. My journey towards healing myself gained momentum.

So instead of slowly deteriorating as the prognosis for MS goes, I've been slowly taking back what was lost. It is an amazing process and one that's likely to continue for a long time. It's a spiritual truth that when you've first awakened, you can't go back to sleep – and now that I've started healing my life, I find it impossible to go back to just accepting deterioration.

The affirmation of Day Two caused a similar reaction. *I honor the commitments to myself and others.* When I did the exercises in *Anatomy of the Spirit*, I had worked hard to be completely, devastatingly truthful. This was a good experience to have now, because my first instinct was to shrug and say "of course," but then there was that little voice piping up "No, you're not!" Oh? I wasn't? Or maybe I just shied away from commitments? Nah, I tend to keep my word. To others. But what about myself? Hmm, maybe not that good after all. I kept the commitments that just skimmed around on the surface, but any commitments to be thorough didn't last long. After all, what had I done after I read *Anatomy of the Spirit*? Not much, actually. I'd read some other books, but had I done the exercises suggested in these books? Ehh, not really. This was beginning to get embarrassing, and I'd only gone through two days. I was thrilled. It felt like I was finally breaking through a barrier.

What were my values? I'd always appreciated honesty, and I consider myself an honest person, but in all honesty I had to admit that I wasn't entirely truthful towards myself at all times. I did my best to imagine that my MS wasn't there. I figured that the less I thought about it, the better off I was, and in some ways that's true. I had no interest in becoming one of those nightmares I'd seen all too often, those people who use their illness to control their environment, who live for their disease. I really didn't want my slowly deteriorating health to rule my life.

What I wanted most of all was to find the golden key that would unlock the secret treasure chest, where I'd find whatever was needed to cure me. I wanted clarity. Full, complete, total clarity. Within me and around me. Then came the clutter clearing of the Soul Coaching program. I loved it, I clutter cleared for clarity almost everywhere, and released as much as I could manage. *Love it, use it, or get rid of it!* I tried to put as much as possible into the latter category, but there was obviously much I loved, as I still had loads of stuff – sweet postcards with darling messages, kids' drawings, mementos and trinkets – in addition to my fabrics and art supplies. Clutter clearing is an ongoing process and one I might never finish, because I do love my stuff. I love beautiful things, but I have found I'm able to release some things. Plus, it does get easier with time.

I have a "happy" box in which I place the cards that make my heart soar whenever I read them, the drawings my kids have made for me that melt me completely, loving notes my husband leaves, the little things that remind me of especially happy times – and then I use that happy box whenever I'm a bit down. If I'm low and feel underneath the soles of my shoes one day, then I pick out the happy box and read through all the cards and letters. I touch the trinkets and look at the drawings and suddenly life isn't half bad at all. It's like having a gas station for good emotions, a place I can go to top up the tank when I need to. And those other things? Those that don't fit in that box and which I really see no need to keep? They're released while I send a loving thought, a blessing, to the person who sent or gave it to me.

Over the years I've become acutely aware of the wonderful energy of blessings. Blessings that come from the heart are a blessing indeed. Both to the sender and the receiver. It feels good to want the best for everyone, even those who seem to be our adversaries. Because we're all one. I'd heard "we're all one" floating around in the ether, but I'd never experienced it before doing the Soul Journeys we did as part of the Soul Coach training. Not only once, but several times I drifted off to feel that glorious Oneness with all of Creation, from the smallest quarks to the greatest galaxies. And now I see that quantum physics is telling us the same story. It is such a wonderful feeling to have these experiences validated by science, and brings a smile to my face.

I bless the scientists for these discoveries, and I bless myself and the journey I'm on. I can wholeheartedly state that if I hadn't become seriously ill, I would never have traveled inwards and started to listen. I bless the gifts my MS has brought me, and I thank it for the contribution. It's really been a blessing in disguise, because there's no way I want to be without the experiences I've had because of it. Well, aside from the being ill part; the periods I lost my eyesight and such. I could've done without that. No kidding.

So, what did I learn from Soul Coaching? I learned to listen! I learned to not only accept, but to cherish that little voice inside and to listen to my own emotions. My soul talks to me through emotions and feeling good tells me that I'm on the right track. This is a valuable asset as I continue on my healing journey, trying out new therapies. I read about something, close my eyes, and *listen*. Feels good? Try it! So now I'm teaching myself EFT (Emotional Freedom Techniques), and my spine tingles with anticipation when I think of the possibilities. Combining EFT and Soul Coaching? Feels very good!

Many times I've been asked what kind of advice I would pass on to other people with MS, or chronic illnesses in general, and to me these are the most important points:

- *Accept the diagnosis, not the prognosis* ~ Prognoses are based on how people did in the past. This is now, and a heightened awareness makes everything possible. Even miracles!

- *Adopt an Attitude of Gratitude ~* There's loads to be thankful for, even in the midst of chronic disease. Be grateful and give blessings; it makes a world of difference.

- *Forgive ~* Forgive everybody, also yourself.

- *Blessings often come disguised ~* Could you turn your health challenge into something positive – could you use it to get to know yourself better, and learn to listen to your soul's whispers? Invest time in yourself.

- *Share ~* Shared sorrow is half sorrow, but most importantly, shared joy, shared love, is double love. Don't forget to love and live life.

Soul Coaching has allowed me to live a better life with MS by listening to the whispers of my soul. And as a Soul Coach, I'd be delighted to help and guide you to do the same.

∾

CATHERINE TURNER
Victoria, B.C., Canada

CATHERINE TURNER has spent her lifetime in the pursuit of knowledge. Holistic health, visualization, spiritualism, essential oils, numerology, decluttering/organizing, and Feng Shui are a few of the subjects she has explored extensively. Her development is an ongoing pursuit. After years of assisting others with their growth she is successfully experiencing *entelechy* in her own life.

Catherine is certified in Reiki, Geo Tran, Soul Coaching® and Past Life Regression. She is also a Laughter Yoga Teacher, practicing in Victoria, B.C., Canada. For consultations, lectures, workshops and classes contact Catherine at awms2008@shaw.ca

Acceptance

CATHERINE TURNER

Unexpected life changes can lead to amazing adventures!

After listening to a radio program discussing how middle-class families were "one paycheck away from losing their homes," unfortunately I too found myself buying into this widespread financial fear. I remember confiding this anxiety to someone at the time, "I'm afraid my life is going to be whipped out from underneath me."

Shortly afterwards, not only did the world's financial security crumble, but so too did my own financial security. I was forced to close the doors to one business, but, as so often happens, I also began to slowly open the doors to a new career, one for which I'd had a particular passion for many years.

I was not growing any younger and a change for my life was in the air. For years lurking in the background was my dream to open the doors to a healing practice where I could share my growing knowledge of the holistic arts. With my son now an adult, perhaps now was the time to begin a new journey. So I began to expand my holistic studies.

One of the books I came across was *Soul Coaching*, by Denise Linn. Where had this book been hiding? This was just what I was looking for! In my former professional background, clutter had certainly made me crazy. And, as Denise explains so well, clutter outside reflects clutter inside. What an amazing 28 day journey I had through that book. I quickly realized that this was something I wanted to pursue professionally in the future. After a search on the Internet, I discovered that Denise Linn taught a Soul Coaching and Past Life Regression Certification Training.

Becoming a Soul Coach

I knew that what Denise offered in her training would tie together everything that I had believed and practiced for over thirty years. It felt right to attend this training, so I telephoned the office on a weekend expecting to leave a message. Much to my surprise, Denise answered the phone. She told me that the next program had been full but that someone had just cancelled. I could have their spot if I wanted it! I took these two things as signs that I was meant to take the program. Unexpected life changes can lead to amazing adventures!

I clearly remember my first day at Summerhill Ranch, Denise's home and training site. I was sitting in the hot tub in the morning and took a picture of what appeared to be a dancing angel cloud. I truly felt as though all the angels in the heavens were smiling down upon me. When I showed this picture to Denise she agreed it looked just like a dancing lady. A few days later when Denise announced her upcoming Imagery Dance Workshop, I knew this was not going to be my only adventure at Summerhill Ranch!

My Soul Coaching training progressed very quickly. Each day was a new adventure and deeper learning experience, with tools to add to my teaching toolbox. One of those tools was the making of a Spirit Stick. Little did I know that this was to become an important turning point for me. As we began our Spirit Stick creations, I felt very self-conscious and awkward. I struggled at times due to limited use of my right hand and felt overwhelmed because of a long-held belief that I wasn't an artistic person. At some level I must have responded to the sacred and safe environment Denise had co-created at Summerhill. So I felt encouraged and supported to try this exercise anyway.

I successfully completed my Spirit Stick. In fact it turned out to be very symbolic. It represented my belief system surrounding Nature, incorporating the four directions, the four elements, the body chakras, a central core, and also my son. For me this Spirit Stick represented the essence of *me* and what I believe in, as well as my experience of that moment. The stick was approximately a foot and a half tall with several smaller branches. One particular branch near the bottom curved out and around, like a mother hen with her wings spread out, gathering her chicks to protect her brood. To me this symbolized the way Denise Linn gathers and protects all of her students.

After completing my Spirit Stick, I set it aside on a table top, thinking it would be safe. A fellow classmate, who was apparently a little clumsy, somehow knocked my stick onto the tiled floor. Although I was not in the immediate room, I witnessed the aftermath and was devastated. Picking up the treasured pieces of my Spirit Stick, I walked outside, upset and traumatized. This stick had meant so much to me on so many levels! As I carried my broken treasure outside, I wondered what lessons this accident held for me.

But as I walked up the pathway to the Lodge I felt something click within me. I suddenly found myself wondering, "Do I really want to continue with this anger, frustration, and victimhood?" Suddenly, I began to laugh, great gales of laughter!

I turned around smiling, and strolled back down the path, whistling a happy tune. I found myself walking over to the burn pile and just stood there in front of it for a while. Even while I was creating my Spirit Stick I had known that I would not be able to bring it home because it wouldn't fit in my carry-on-bag anyway. I now cradled this stick in my arms, as you would a baby, and in a sense, watched it grow to full maturity. We had both graduated and were now ready to move on with our individual adventures in life.

I looked at the stick one last time and thanked it for the valuable lessons it had taught me. Then, ceremoniously, I tossed it onto the burn pile so that it could go back to Mother Earth, as if it were a child being given wings, allowed to fly on its own at last. Three months later, my son announced to me that he and his girlfriend had made the decision to get married!

Later, when I was talking with Denise one-on-one about the incident she said, "It sounds like acceptance to me, Cathy."

I agreed with her. "Yes," I said, "This was an amazing example of acceptance." I felt very calm and solid; I also felt acknowledged and understood. I thought, "Wow, *acceptance*. It can be this simple. Hmmm, acceptance may not always be this easy, but it *can* be simple!" This was just one of many powerful lessons that were in store for me during this training. Denise provides so many avenues for her students to grow, and in turn, enables each of them to pass these learnings on to their students. When I returned home from Summerhill, that feeling of acceptance stayed with me.

Another experience that helped me to grow in my understanding of the power of clutter clearing in Soul Coaching came when I applied my expertise in this field to Denise's pantry. As students, everyone participates in the chores surrounding the meals, including setting the table and cleaning up afterwards. With so many hands in the pantry, things don't always make their way back to their proper storage area. I took on some of this organizational responsibility, quietly and without fanfare.

Acceptance

AFFIRMATION: *I unconditionally accept, cherish, and love myself just as I am.*

Acceptance is a sacred act of power. Accept your light! Embrace all parts of yourself! Allow yourself to receive the gifts of the universe. You're worthy of these blessings and so much more.

That was until one of the other students came in one morning and, for the first time, saw the beautiful elephant tapestry that hung at the end of this long room. Suddenly she realized that it was my clutter clearing that had brought its beauty to light. She had not noticed this tapestry before, even though it had always been there. She thanked me in front of the entire group and everyone acknowledged that this was the amazing power of clutter clearing in action. My intent had only been to provide a *thank you* for Denise, but all benefited from the lesson of the calm and clarity that good organization can bring.

The 28 Day program coaches your inner and outer clutter to be released and/or returned to its proper place. As a Soul Coach, I am now able to teach my students to let their Soul Light shine more clearly, just as I enabled all the candle holders in Denise's pantry to shine more brightly, to give off their light more clearly. Each of us has an inner light that shines purely when we buff and polish our personal Soul.

Two weeks after completing my Soul Coaching Certification Training, I returned to California to participate in the Weekend of Miracles Course. I knew I wanted to learn all I could from Denise. This dynamic weekend not only provided a more in-depth learning experience, I also met many other past students and was able to train with graduates from several of her other programs. What a wonderfully safe and welcoming environment it was! I admired Denise's positive attitude and grace. And she was a perfect example for me because we shared similar life experiences. She had risen above all challenges to become a successful wife, mother and business woman who works with and respects nature. She'd achieved great success in the same goals I'd also been working on.

Laughter Yoga Teacher Certification
My quest for meaning and new avenues of employment continued when I went to a Laughter Yoga Certification Course. I had been introduced to a woman several months earlier and she had discussed with me the possibility of opening up a Laughter Yoga club. She wanted me to join her in this venture and suggested that I visit the website. I was very interested in what I saw and wondered if I could become involved with this practice as part of a new business. I was also keenly interested in the health benefits of Laughter Yoga.

I discovered that the founder, Dr. Madan Kataria from India, was coming to Canada, not far from where I live. I took this as a sign and registered for the course. There were several other positive signs, such as their holding my spot and allowing me to pay when I arrived. I had some doubts about whether this was for real but I felt the signs were there and after all, what did I have to lose?

The course lasted for a week and we laughed on and off for approximately eight hours every day. I can tell you that there were times when this became extremely overwhelming. However, the end result was that I felt happy and knew that this program would incorporate nicely into my Soul Coaching training.

There were many similarities between Denise Linn's courses and the Laughter Yoga training. Both were held outside; the weather was warm; the food was healthy and tasted great. People were there because they really *wanted* to be there. The whole atmosphere felt safe. A huge *aha* moment came for me during the breath training. Laughter Yoga includes several different laughter breathing exercises and it seems that over the years, I had already been intuitively doing these on my own!

Imagery Dance
It felt as though my life was truly beginning to fall into place. My spiritual journey had been furthered because I was now asking deeper questions. I was steadily working to discover just what I wanted to believe in, and how that could be put to use in creatively exploring a new career – one that it appeared was being placed

at my feet. Life took on new meaning; my soul was singing, and my heart beat to a new rhythm. I could see a bright and shining future emerging, through helping others to heal and grow.

And so I was ready to again return to Summerhill Ranch in the Fall and experience my third, again very different, training with Denise Linn called Imagery Dance. In all of her programs, Denise teaches the importance of movement. Her love of movement is so strong that there is a purpose-built Dance Barn at her ranch. It was such an honor and so exciting to be part of the very first time this Dance Barn would be initiated, along with the movement of intent bodies, swirling individually and as one!

The teachings in this program encourage and engage the multi-levels of our body to move naturally through the sound and spirit of music. By now I had a deep trust in Denise as an instructor and spiritual teacher. I was still searching for a way to fully integrate all of this new material into my life and to put together a new career that would provide meaningful work, growing within myself, and helping others to grow. These courses were all different parts of my journey, my evolution. But by putting these teachings together, I knew I'd be better able to teach others a more fulfilling way to live, while developing a new holistic practice for myself as well as a new career.

Through the Imagery Dance course I became much more in touch with my femininity, which allowed my creativity to easily expand and rise to the surface. While at Summerhill, I went to visit the burn pile to see if my Spirit Stick was still there. Like a child who had left home, I was looking forward to a visit. And there it was, waiting for my return! With much gentle poking and prodding I was able to retrieve it. I photographed it from many different angles. And when I was done, I placed it in one of the many mole holes near the art studio on the ranch. I felt complete.

Learning to Accept
In spite of the sudden life and career changing episodes of my recent past, I was blessed to be able to attend Denise's retreats and witness her living from a place of acceptance. Although it had taken her years to resolve some of the more painful matters in her life, it was the process of acceptance that had allowed her to come to a place of peace. Through sharing her life experiences, Denise enriched my life, and as a role model, showed me a way to use my own life-changing experiences to assist others in creating positive change in their lives as well.

Just like Denise, my life experiences had led me on a journey to acceptance, and now I was finally able to enrich the lives of others. I discovered that creating a safe environment greatly assists in the healing process and that when we can simply relax, healing occurs much more rapidly. I have now stepped forward to create a safe healing place for my own clients.

Today I incorporate each one of my learning experiences into my daily life. It is simply a decision, like the one I made with my Spirit Stick at Summerhill – to accept that it was a *physical* thing that broke, and not my *Spirit*. It required letting go, much like we let our children go to find their own way in the world. Ask yourself, what do I want to accept into my life, with every thought, with every word, with every deed? If you don't know the answer yet, don't give up. Keep going; keep asking the questions. The answers will burn more brightly for you each day. All answers become clearer for us all, as more and more of the weighted clutter clears from our lives.

During the process of my healing journey I was fortunate enough to discover and sign up for Soul Coaching. While there, through many Vision Journeys, I realized that the magnificent sacred oak on the property at Summerhill Ranch had been calling to me for years. I was finally able to answer that call, hug the mighty oak and learn the practice of Soul Coaching. This journey was a reminder to me of the joy and simplicity of how I had lived my life a long time ago. The discipline of the 28 day program assisted me in a profound way to return to those earlier days of ease. It helped me to cleanse my inner spiritual body and learn to manifest joy in my outer life.

I learned how to heal the polarity of the personal and financial turmoil that surrounded me, after the life I had known had been suddenly whipped out from under me. I was able to explore all the solid trainings contained within Soul Coaching, Past Life Regression, Weekend of Miracles, and Imagery Dance with Denise Linn. Each one of them reinforced my ability to walk forward with complete acceptance of *who I am*, and to grow. Then when I saw the powerful healing potential of combining Laughter Yoga with these amazing techniques I knew I was truly ready, willing and able to assist others to clear their inner and outer clutter, in order to cleanse their Soul, enabling them to walk tall into positive futures.

I invite you to come grow with me!

Believe

*AFFIRMATION: The best
is yet to come!*

*Believe in yourself!
Have faith in magic and miracles.
If you can conceive it,
you can achieve it.*

MISASHA
Canada

MISASHA – THE SAGE SPIRIT, a.k.a. J. Gean Hemming, continues to live life experientially. An adventurer and world traveler, she has been from Greenland to Australia – and many places in between – Machu Picchu, Mexico, Ireland. . . . She holds a degree in English and Psychology and has flown in two Angel Derbys (All Women's International Air Races). She is filled with gratitude for support from Mighty Forces as well as the daily whisperings from her Soul. She is trying her vigilant best to not let any static interfere with reception!

Volunteering at a day-long workshop by Denise Linn in April 2006 led her to Denise's next Soul Coaching® training – SC17. There was one spot left, but that was all she needed! Her life and the lives of many around her have been strengthened as a result.

A near-death experience at age 20, life's opportunities-for-growth, chosen learnings, and a love of books have all helped mould her perception of life . . . and the here-after. Resolution and details of her current dark-night-of-the-soul will be forthcoming. She's not quite sure when or in what format, but she has a heaping-helping of Faith to sustain her!!

Her affirmation: Let Right Prevail. Thy Will be done. "Let Right Prevail" is the motto of the Law Society of Upper Canada.

Contact: TheSageSpirit@gmail.com

Saying YES to Life
... in Spite of *Seeming* Impossibilities

MISASHA

When you feel like you're being-put-through-the-wringer,
please understand that it just means you're worth laundering.

"Are you taking antidepressants?"
The question astounded me!
"No," I told the psychic and clairvoyant counselor, who had quickly impressed me with her *knowing*. "I'm resilient."
"You must be!
I see people all the time who have lost far less than you, and they simply cannot cope!"
I reflected on her comment. What lets one person seemingly *go-with-the-flow, roll-with-the-punches,* and *when-knocked-down-seven-get-up-eight* – more easily than another? Why, so often, do we butt our heads against what *is,* become frozen in fear, and begin thinking that life is just one *vicious* cycle . . . and perhaps isn't worth living at all?

Why was it, after the crash of the stock market during the Roaring '20s, that so many people, having lost all their material assets, felt they had nothing left to live for? Suicide rates dramatically increased during and after this event. Why do we mistakenly believe that what is *out there* has control over us; that our personal power resides in external circumstances, in someone, or something beyond ourselves? Our first instinct is to retreat or withdraw in fear. Through my experiences and those of others, I know this type of thinking is not based on truth!

Denise Linn's autobiography, *If I Can Forgive So Can You,* is inspiring, heartrending, and uplifting. She unfolds childhood experiences that caused her to believe at seventeen that she *deserved* to be shot by an unknown assailant, because she was *unworthy.* Reclaiming her personal power was not easy but she did it! Eventually she rewrote her personal history to no longer see herself as a victim. Her destiny, as a result, was forever changed for the better. Denise is the wise, compassionate mentor and teacher to over four hundred Soul Coaches that she has trained and certified. I am grateful and blessed to be counted within this number. Like the first pebble tossed into a still millpond, her teachings have rippled out globally, and her trained Soul Coaches now share light and hope around the world. As Denise continues to teach and train new Soul Coaches each year, the vibration of the planet rises. A prolific author, Denise's books are available in over twenty languages. *Facing Fear/Embracing Faith* is one Soul Coaching teaching that has prominence in *my* life.

Many of us find ourselves in circumstances over which we have no control. Consider Viktor Frankl; he spent three years in Nazi concentration camps. What allowed Frankl to survive? How was he different from those imprisoned with him? Why and how did he retain his will to live – when countless others felt hopeless, helpless, lost their wills to live, and perished?

Within days of Frankl's release, he told a friend: "I must tell you, that when all this happens to someone, to be tested in such a way, that it must have some meaning. I have a feeling – and I don't know how else to say it – that something waits for me. That something is expected of me, that I am destined for something." And, so he was!

Frankl's book, *Man's Search for Meaning* was dictated in nine days. It sold nine million copies over fifty years, and has been translated into twenty-four languages. Inspired, he went on to develop *Logotherapy*. *Logos* is a Greek word that denotes *meaning*. Denise says: "We can't always choose the circumstances of our life, but we *can* choose the meaning we give those events." Since meaning does not depend on either circumstances or on particular events, what then keeps us imprisoned in our past, or longing for the land of "Someday – I'll . . . ?" What prevents us from embracing life in the *now*? Fear? For example, fear of failure may make you feel the need to have all your ducks neatly lined up before taking action. This sort of resistance to faith creates stress or panic when one duck falls out of the lineup. Your soul, however, does not live in fear; it never has; it never will!

Your soul's constant whisperings are overpowered by the static created by your *judge-interpreter*. You may recognize the *judge-interpreter* as your super-reasonable, working-the-will ego-mind which gives adrenalin-pumping *meaning* to your experiences. For example, before February 2001, I worked my will in the Network Marketing Industry, astonishing the masses with my byline: over-under-around-or-through . . . failure-is-not-an-option!

Goethe's prophetic words: *Be bold and Mighty Forces will come to your aid,* offered a challenging alternative. There was a resonant quality to Goethe's words that I could feel and which moved me in an inexplicable way. I now know that it was my soul resonating with truth, though my *judge-interpreter* found the notion rather intimidating. Surrendering so fully in Faith was not only an alien concept, but disempowering! Life, however, was to benevolently settle the matter, and grant me an opportunity to give Goethe's intriguing proclamation a *test-of-fire.*

My new friend Jill wanted to reach a personal goal in her network-marketing business. Coincidentally, it was the same goal that I achieved, to the amazement of onlookers, in my first full month with the same Network Marketing Company. Jill's situation, however, would not be the adrenaline-generating, working-the-will endeavor that mine was, some four years earlier. Jill would not have the highly-placed humans or the power-hungry driven minds, from two countries, to help her. She just had me as her mentor, our joint Faith and the much anticipated *Mighty Forces,* promised by Goethe.

To reach her goal, Jill and her team needed US$24,000 in sales, in one month! The deadline was midnight, February 28, 2001, the shortest month of the year! As I scrutinized her team's performance from January and December, my *judge-interpreter* predicted that she was clearly not even in the running! Indeed, it did look impossible for Jill's team to reach US$24,000 . . . realistically . . . humanly *impossible*! It wasn't surprising that Jill's up-line leaders labeled her a non-contender. "What is she thinking?! How does she expect her team to sell US$24,000 in February? December sales were only US$2825 and January sales not much better at US$3440?" sneered my *judge-interpreter.*

Indeed, not one entrepreneur was on Jill's team; most were merely users of the products.

I had to remind myself that I was *testing* Goethe's words and that I must be bold and trusting so that *Mighty Forces* would come to our aid. And so, despite my *judge-interpreter's* all-knowing-failure-forecast, I pledged my commitment to help. I had not met Jill's husband when I moved into their spare bedroom for the month. Don, a very successful businessman seemed content to *let the little woman do her thing;* and although I knew it would be easier with his support, I made no attempt to recruit him.

That month sped by and at midnight, February 28 Jill and I anxiously checked her *stats.* Her 18-member team had tripled, now numbering 54. By now Don even had Jill's website boldly emblazoned on the tailgate of his macho black truck! Month-end total sales – as I rubbed my disbelieving eyes – were US$24,001!!

"Imagine! Just imagine!" I was in a euphoric state of shocked disbelief . . . 24000 and *one!* Goethe's words were true! Faith *can* work miracles! I was filled with gratitude! The next day one of Jill's highly placed up-line leaders, still shaking her head in disbelief asked me "How did you pull *that* one off?!" I told her that we used a seven-point game-plan . . . *The Seven Spiritual Laws of Success,* by Deepak Chopra. "Yes, yes, I know," she impatiently replied, "But how did you *really* do it?" Jill and I only smiled.

Perception: before you can recognize a miracle, first you must *believe* in miracles. Faith, teamwork, trust, being bold, and taking a risk, made the humanly impossible *possible*! Jill just wanted to do *good*, and I had no *vested interest* in her success; as a result, *Mighty Forces* came to our aid. It was that simple, it was that unbelievable, and yet it was true! Surrendering to Faith was a unique and gratifying experience!

That month was delightful and fun – so unlike my adrenaline-generating achievement, some four years earlier. Don splurged, organizing a huge congratu-latory surprise-party, even having an oversized sign created, thanking me. Some of Jill's friends asked her what I was getting out of it. "Nothing," she said. Finan-cially that was true; but what I got, though not tangible, was a priceless gift. My life would never be the same. My perception on how goals could be achieved was shattered. With exquisite finesse, and in dramatic fashion, *one* dollar disproved my *judge-interpreter's* all-knowing-failure-forecast. *One* dollar was the compelling evidence that proved Goethe correct.

Experiencing the results of faith and having *Mighty Forces* come to my aid was absolutely . . . delicious! This was how I wanted to experience life! Life is not a vicious-cycle of events and of circumstances, to be judged with fearful trepida-tion, or in working one's will. No! Life is a *delicious-cycle* – to be savored, enjoyed, and replayed – when encouragement is most needed! Jill, listening to *her* soul's whisperings, is now selling teddy bears in Florida!

Life is choice. Choose to *take back your power!*
Tip: Choose to explore what fears are stopping you from moving forward. Know that no one is immune to fear. Fears that you do not face will continue to persist. James Baldwin noted, "Not everything that is faced can be changed, but nothing can be changed until it is faced."

Make a list of things that you are afraid of. Write: "I am afraid of _____," and be very specific. From your list, select your biggest fear and consider what might be the absolute worst outcome. Remember, fears do not make you who you are, they are *just* fears. Using your creativity, discover how you can not only overcome these fears, but can actually flourish.

Each step you take towards conquering your fear reduces its hold on you. Move beyond your known, your status quo, your comfort zone, and take a risk! If, for example, public speaking terrifies you, you might choose to join a toastmaster's group; your self-confidence will grow with each action-step you take. Start small and build; it is a process. Fear of failure only serves to paralyze your life. Define fear by what it most often is, *F*alse *E*vidence *A*ppearing *R*eal! Consider the emo-tional high when Babe Ruth set the world's record for most home runs hit. Most don't know but Ruth also holds the record for most strike-outs! In baseball, as in life, those most willing to risk failure are those most likely to succeed. Success builds upon success.

Meaning comes from within you . . . no one but you holds the pen that writes *your* storyline. Not only do you hold the pen, you also dictate the story. But, it's not your soul dictating. The soul whispers to you, always urging you to do what is for your greatest joy and well-being. If this concept comes as new information, rejoice! Consider the powerful gift of *choice* that you now have.

By gaining new awareness, you can *choose* to alter your perceptions that give emotionally-charged meaning to your history. Remember, your *judge-interpreter* creates the static that prevents you from hearing your soul's whispers. The expression, *knowledge is power* is not true. In truth, it is only *potential* power. Unused, it is impotent. You may have heard, *Knowledge not used is knowledge wasted.* A Zen saying sums it up as, *To know and not to do is not to know.*

Regardless of how deeply rutted or grooved your old records and tapes may be, new information can bring new perceptions. The conviction of Logotherapy is that no situation is without potential for a *seed of meaning.* Renewed perceptions can open your inner ear to your soul's whispers.

Consider this: if we author events that do not uplift, encourage, or empower our lives – then let's change that! Fears neither uplift, nor encourage, nor empower. If the story that your *judge-interpreter* created about your history doesn't give your day a happiness-boost, it's time to *delete, rewrite, reframe* or *transmute* that old storyline. For, it is *not* a story dictated by your soul!

A modern day parable: A man was ambling along a quiet country road. Over the next rise he saw a farm. As he approached, he could hear singing, humming and whistling. His steps quickened . . . anxious to view the joy-filled scene behind the little red barn. Anticipation mounted as he rounded the corner. His eyes did a swift survey, and he stood frozen in stunned and speechless perplexity. How quite unlikely, he thought. The scene made no sense to him. It was just too bizarre for his reasoning mind to rationally interpret. And, to him, it made no sense whatsoever!

There before him, so engrossed in the task at hand that she didn't even notice his presence, was the source of all the merriment. It was a young girl, humming away as she happily hoisted yet another shovelful of manure. With obvious delight she was actually enjoying the task! His eyes finally gave way to his tongue. "You seem so happy, and for the life of me, I really cannot understand why. Will you explain to me, why shoveling manure makes you so cheerful? What pleasure are you getting from shoveling *manure*? It's such a huge pile, and you're such a little girl. It may take you days to shovel out the barn!"

Without pausing or missing a shovelful, she just grinned broadly. Shoveling more furiously, she laughed, "Well, with all this 'poop', there's just gotta' be a pony in here somewhere!!"

All it takes is the seed of a meaning, and it's *Faith* that gives life meaning. Our *judge-interpreter* keeps us trapped in the past or looking wistfully to the future. Both instances siphon energy gifted for today. Misery does love company. My suggestion: leave misery to wallow alone in its own negative vibration; and consider the perception that the *judge-interpreter*, within the man in the parable, gave to the little girl shoveling manure.

Your birth was not an accident, regardless of what you may have been told. My mom said "It's a miracle he lived!" when I told her my ex was born three months after his seventeen-year-old mother and nineteen-year-old father married. *Mumsie's* life was not without challenges – her dad died when she was eighteen, and she took on the responsibilities of helping raise two younger siblings. Nonetheless, she never lost her sense of humor. Humor brings healing to your body, joy to your spirit, and a smile to your soul. You are here, at this time in humanity's evolution – *on purpose.* There will never be born another *you* – a person with the same combination of gifts, talents, and qualities that only you possess. Not even if you are an identical twin! You are unique! Enjoyment of life is your birthright!

> ## Miracles
>
> *AFFIRMATION: My life is a miracle!*
>
> *Miracles occur in your life every day. Watch for and embrace them. As you notice and accept the small wonders in your life, greater gifts will grow in abundance all around you.*

Ask yourself, what is keeping me from being happy? If you quiet your static, listen closely, you just may hear your soul whispering . . . "Story-lines from your past can't resonate, or vibrate with happy. Fear vibrates at a very low frequency." For example, consider you have three tuning forks. Two are tuned to 'C' note; the third is tuned to 'B' note. When 'B' is struck, it begins to vibrate. But, it vibrates alone. When one of the 'C' forks is struck, it too begins to vibrate. But, it is *not* alone. The third fork soon recognizes the vibrational frequency. It says, "I recognize that frequency; it's just like mine!" Now both 'C' forks vibrate in har-mony and in unison. As you *delete, rewrite, reframe,* or *transmute* . . . your entire being can begin to vibrate in harmony with higher frequencies . . . frequencies like optimism, confidence, hope, inner-strength, faith, resiliency, self-sufficiency, contentment, joy . . . the list is endless.

A Truth: Change never visits alone; Fear and Chaos are its closest allies. But, Fear is part of life, and *everyone* feels it. Fear does not realize that Faith is its twin brother. They are just opposite sides of the same coin. The mind cannot hold two opposing thoughts at one time; neither can both sides of a coin be seen at the same time. You cannot have happy and sad thoughts simultaneously; choose which side of the coin *you* wish to experience.

Choose to flip the coin, for you are never deprived of choice, even if you do nothing – that is still a choice! Expand boundaries-that-limit by embracing Faith. It is not possible to say YES to life . . . in spite of *seeming* impossibilities . . . without a heaping-helping-of-Faith. A knowing-ness, at the very core of your being, that gives you assurance you are not alone and *will* be supported if you but *ask.*

A Truth: You have *never* been alone, nor will you ever be! Remember the $1 that changed my life forever, that February? Faith is likened to the knowing-ness of the bird, which begins singing during dawn's darkest hour; within she *feels* the light and her joy is neither restrained, nor can it be contained.

For example, in November 2006, external circumstances, over which I had no control, drew me into a legal matter. I chose to stand strong in my *knowing* of what was right and just, and to speak the truth – while others did not. I refused to allow coercion or intimidation to take away my personal power. Self-represented, I told the Ontario Provincial Court that I fervently believe that those in positions of influence, trust and perceived external-power must adhere to an acceptable level of truth and integrity. "Amen to that!" said the Judge. However, only partial judgment was awarded me, since *arguments* cannot be presented or evidence weighed during summary judgment hearings – that's the role for a trial judge.

Truth, I know, always seeks the light-of-day, and my resolve and faith is strengthened by Psalm 127–1: *Except the Lord builds the house, they labor in vain that build it.* Has this been easy? No, not at all; dark-nights-of-the-soul *never* are. Briefings and storylines, created by persons in positions of trust, influence, and perceived external-power resulted in estrangements with some family members, friends, and professional acquaintances. My previously impeccable credit rating remains severely damaged; financial institutions cancelled several of my credit cards in early 2007. Further, I had no choice but to sell my townhouse in June 2007.

I even converted a Registered Retirement Savings Plan to a Life Income Fund, expecting to free-up funding for my first independent documentary film in Peru – mid-June 2007. All was set . . . waiting only for my funds and the final flight details. Regrettably the conversion-payout unexpectedly fell short of the promised amount, and I was forced to abort the project with less than two weeks prior to departure for the shoot!

As my simmering, seething *judge-interpreter's* self-righteous-indignation mellowed, softened and finally surrendered to my soul's quiet urgings, I finally heard my soul whisper*: there is no loss in Divine mind.* And so, my faith was re-fortified and I hold even stronger now. The fiercer winds blow, the deeper trees send down roots. I take another lesson from trees that bend in the gale, like the palm, and do not break.

Roman Emperor and philosopher Marcus Aurelius (121–180 AD) provides words of truth: "We shrink from change; yet is there anything that can come into being without it? What does Nature hold dearer; or more proper to herself? Could you have a hot bath unless the firewood underwent some change? Do you not see, then, that change in yourself is of the same order, and no less necessary to Nature?"

Faith can come from learning the stories of others who have overcome *seeming* impossibilities, stories both factual (e.g. Denise Linn and Frankl) and mythical. Every 500 years, the phoenix burns itself on a funeral pyre. It then rises from the ashes for another cycle – rejuvenated, revitalized and with youthful vitality. Remember too, it is through firing that steel is strengthened.

I believe my experience, that February so long ago, was preparing me for my current *firing* in *life's crucible* . . . which is not yet concluded. Know that as you begin to empower yourself, your strength and Faith will ripple out across this vast universe. You may never know whose life you have been destined to positively impact, as your Faith allows you to move beyond your limitations. I *know* the February miracle was primarily for my learning as it now supports my present life-challenge. Faith is the mainstay, the major foundational support in my life. It causes some folks to shake their heads in disbelief while others ask questions like, "Are you taking antidepressants?"

When you feel like you're being-put-through-the-wringer, please understand that it just means you're worth laundering. Buddha reminds us: "You yourself, as much as anybody in the entire universe, deserve your love and affection."

Practice daily self-care and always remember: Life is *not* a vicious-cycle; it is a delicious-cycle! May your life be blessed in this knowing.

Faith

*AFFIRMATION: My life
is divinely guided.*

*Trust that you're exactly where you
need to be. Have faith in yourself and
know that you're divinely guided . . .
even when you have doubts. Believe!
You've planted your seeds, now allow
the Creator to do the rest.*

DEBORAH JANELLE SMITH

San Francisco, California, USA

DEBORAH IS CURRENTLY LIVING in San Ramon, on the east Bay of San Francisco, California, where she relocated in February 2008. Deborah frequently travels between California and Queensland. Deborah is continuing her journey in life through her passion of helping others through Soul Coaching© and with her Dragon Boat Paddling. As the USA distributor of Merlin Dragon Boat Paddles, Deborah attends dragon boat regattas and festivals, throughout the USA promoting Merlin paddles and gear. Deborah has created a deck of *Thank You* cards. The cards are to give away with the message of "thanks."

Deborah was born in Maryborough, Queensland, Australia, where she lived for 19 years until relocating to the Sunshine Coast then to Brisbane as a business owner. Deborah's business career includes director and franchisor of an Australia wide business along with her own business as a bookkeeping consultant, assisting small businesses with their bookkeeping and office administration. Deborah is also a MYOB (an Australian Business and Accounting Software Company) professional partner bookkeeper.

Deborah attended Aldridge State High School in Maryborough, before leaving to work at the local newspaper. Deborah has two beautiful children, Danyelle and Bradley.

Deborah may be contacted via her Merlin Dragon Boat website as a Soul Coach™ at www.MerlinGearUSA.com

Email Deborah@MerlinGearUSA.com

Journey of the Soul

DEBORAH JANELLE SMITH

*The universe will take care of us when we operate unconditionally
and give without expectation.*

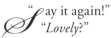"ay it again!"
"*Lovely?*"
"Yes say it again, I just love hearing you say that word. I could listen to you all day. Love your accent!"
"But, I don't have an accent!"
I'm paddling away, saying over and over again "lovely" . . .
"Yes, say it again."
I am so blessed!
On a beautiful clear day, sky blue, glimmering, shimmering sunshine surrounding us. "Look!" To the left a seal is watching over us, lying so serene and effortless in the warm waters, sharing the Bay with us and our dragon boat. I'm here with a crew of twenty paddlers training for the next competitive race; paddling as *one*; paddling in time, in sync; the entire boat paddling one stroke.

I'm out on the water in California at Berkeley Marina. Friends newly met – wonderful, blissful and peaceful, yet paddling with strength. How did I come to be here? So many people one meets, open and warming to my heart. I'm listening to a song from Errol as he drums the beat on the dash while stopped at traffic lights. How lucky am I? I'm being serenaded by this bus-driving jazz-singing entertainer as he drives me to my destination, uplifting my soul. "Please take this music CD I recorded as a gift" says Errol, as I say my goodbyes till next time. I'm so blessed! Me. Yes me!

Now I'm sitting and waiting. I'm allowing myself time to just sit and be patient; learning to be patient while observing the hurriedness of others around me. I'm waiting. I'm sitting, looking all around me; taking time to befriend the people close by. I'm outside the train station. I'm waiting and listening to another. He too is like me; sitting on the concrete bench. Waiting patiently I listen as he explains to me his day of adventure and turmoil which has left him with no money for the train ride home.

After I take a phone call on my mobile phone, my down-and-out bench-sitting friend asks 'Will you help me reset the ring tone on my phone?" "Of course I will," I reply. "Let me see how I can help," just as he offers me a swig of wine from the bottle encased in a brown paper bag. "No thanks – I don't drink." But I did help with his phone problem. I'm seeing the love in everyone I meet. Again, I'm blessed.

Again, I'm watching, observing and listening to the different languages while riding the train. Well, standing in the train for my short trip from station to station. As I look down, I see curiosity through the eyes of a baby staring up at me in wonder. This baby, maybe a year old is talking to me with feelings of awe through her eyes. I'm having a conversation with this precious baby, direct from her soul through her baby blue inquisitive eyes to me. Inspiring! This baby is so unlike the many other train passengers; most connected via earphones listening to their favorite music, oblivious to noise and activity around them. 'Don't talk to me – I'm occupied with myself' is their message; quite unlike my friend the baby. "I'm inquisitive. I have a need to learn through observing with my senses. I'm communicating with my eyes, just as now. Thank you." These are precious moments to savor.

Back at my first train station . . . across the tracks on Platform Two, my new friend from Peru waves as he awaits his train. From the opposite end, on Platform Two, Shayne gives a big wave to farewell me on my journey. I'm greeted with big smiles, big waves from two souls with special needs. I travel the bus route with them both, then continue my travels in a different direction. I return their smiles and waves. My new friends. My new special friends. I'm blessed, once again.

The bus, the express bus ploughs along with the congested traffic. My conversation in broken English with my companion from Peru, centers on his work and his country. "Very, very cold!" I understand those words, though much of his conversation is difficult to comprehend. My friend from Peru has allowed me to experience another culture, and once again I allow my patience time to sit with him. When the trip is complete his words are always "thank you for talking to me." I'm thankful also; thankful that he chose me to be part of his world on his way home from work.

'I'll be your friend" Shayne assures me. Here is another new acquaintance while waiting at the bus shelter for the bus to arrive. Shayne explains how he was deprived of oxygen when born and now has a disability. So honest about who he is, without judgment. He tells me about the medals he won at the Special Games and how great he is at running. He won Gold! "Great for you Shayne!" This beautiful soul bares all of his life story, full of proud achievements, including his marriage. Shayne is newly married to Arielle. He continues on to tell me about his wedding night and how when he took the garter from Arielle's leg, he accidentally bit her! What a story for a wedding night, as he tells me in great detail of the bruise he left behind. Very open, very loving. Telling the story just how it is, of working at a local supermarket, full of enthusiasm for his job. Thank You Shayne for your openness and being my friend too.

A treat before paddling is a trip to the local coffee shop. "So where are you from? England?" the assistant asks politely. "No, I'm from Australia," I reply. "I just love your accent. I would like to travel to Australia one day," is her response as my order is taken. Such friendly people in this world! I'm lucky again for the open conversations wherever I go, from the coffee shops to the buses and trains. Slowing the business of my life to stop and listen has enriched my every day.

Another grocery store in my area has very special people on staff working in all areas. One such lovely man spoke to me when I was sitting outside the store, before riding my bike home, about how he became so wet. He fell into the shopping center fountain. "How did you do that?" I enquired. "I was just sitting there and I fell back," was his reply. So honest, truthful and without shame. I was concerned he was in wet clothes, but shortly after a manager spoke to him about his little dip! He was well looked after. My heart felt for this young man who was merely taking a break near the water, only to fall in. He was taking his time, looking around, being an observer while working. Hey, observing while working, taking time to listen to the water fountain. How often do I just sit and listen to the water, or the birds singing or the lizards sunning themselves in the garden or the roses opening to bloom with the sunshine? Obviously not while working! Maybe we all need to do this. Stop and listen. Be a sacred observer to life. Stop. Look around and listen.

> ## Voyage
>
> *AFFIRMATION: I am safe and loved no matter where I am.*
>
> *A journey is coming. Rather than staying in a safe harbor, let your sails unfurl to the wind. The universe absolutely knows, cherishes, and protects you as you ride the currents of your life.*

"I'm almost sixty and still searching for who I am," says Marge, as we sit together discussing life and the New Year ahead. "Who are we? Who am I?" Marge is a new found friend; a business lady looking at and reviewing her life, and sharing all that is, after a few weeks of Soul Coaching. "There's so much ahead for me. I'm not looking at the past or what's behind me. I'm looking forward to an even fuller, richer and rewarding life." As we sip our herbal tea, I ask "How have you changed?" With a deep, contemplating sigh she replies. "Peace. I'm at peace – so much peace. I'm aware of what is natural for me. I'm looking at the coincidences that give me joy. I'm not forcing things to happen and the end result is more beautiful – yes more beautiful! I now have humbleness born out of honesty. The honesty of accepting who I am, where I am in my life and the possibility of what is ahead of me. Decisions I've made throughout my life were not always the best decisions, however, I recognize that I am much better off now." Leaning back in her chair, with gently flowing tears, like crystal droplets enlightening her now clearer vision, she continues slowly. "When I think of Soul Coaching, I think of my soul in a community of family, friends and business associates. What a gift! The universe will take care of us when we operate unconditionally and give without expectation."

"My peace is not without passion – the passion of knowing that I'm coming into my own realm of business, personal growth and awareness; to be aware of everything around me and be thankful for my friends." With deep thoughts manifesting through conversation, Marge looks around feeling and sensing the room and the sounds of calming music serenading her sighs. "I feel that this year will be a phenomenal year. My goal is new-found energy, a changed attitude of acceptance leading me safely into my sixtieth year. I realize that I've been walking through life without living it. Looking back, I've had a limited celebration of the joy of my children, my friends and my family, including my work accomplishments."

As we look across the table at each other I ask, "How will you experience joy?" With a smile and tilt of her head Marge explains, "I will walk through life and be aware. I will be vocal. I will dance. I will be creative. I will learn. I will notice all the colors from beige to rainbow in my life. *I believe living one day of fullness is better than living a week of passiveness.* In my house, I've learned to *let go.* I've learned that de-cluttering is like taking the curtains away from my windows to see the world. My physical things have memories, and letting go of *things* is opening my mind. My mantra for this year is to simplify and explore the beauty of the world."

At this point we sit back to pick a Soul Coaching Oracle Card from the deck. Marge shuffles and picks *Essence* and *Simplify.* Her soul is acknowledging and validating her desires. Now after a brief interruption, Marge goes to the depths of her soul to answer more questions, especially this next one. "How difficult is facing the truth?" Repositioning herself in her chair, with another glass of water to quench her voice, Marge replies, "I didn't like who I was. The truth was a disappointment. I realize that past decisions were unwise, probably because I had unclear goals! My relationships. My finances. My career goals. Now I feel satisfied and healthy. I'm happy at home. I'm happy with my friends."

"Life is living simply, so how can we all become so attached to living a complicated life? I listen more. I felt left out," Marge explains. "As a child I was left out at school – but *now* I'm catching up. No matter how independent I was or am, I am allowing myself to be nurtured. I'm now open to receiving all the time – no matter what! I accept from others and request help when I need it. My friends can only be there to support me if I ask for help and they respond. What a gift!"

As if a light bulb appears brilliant and bright, and her consciousness is now illuminated in vibrant light, Marge softly says "I am seeing harmony. I will attract the life I want – Yes . . . attract the life I want." As we discuss *making the universe in harmony with ourselves*, we both agree that we need to be in harmony and in love with ourselves. To love *us*, as we are, and to cherish who we are. For we are *good enough*!

Going deeper within herself and forging to the truth of her soul, Marge says, in a softer, quieter tone "I've learned something *big*; something very big for myself. I have learned how to apologize and that I cannot always be right. I have learned how to speak my mind in a kind and loving manner. What may be important to you may not be to the rest of the world." So, I ask, "Tell me more?"

"Well," Marge continues, "I can give, teach and love with no expectations; either in my work or helping family or friends. It gives me peace and joy." With our thoughts and hearts immersed in our conversation, the night becomes longer and so much more enjoyable. It's always so satisfying, being able to share experiences through sacred conversation embraced by the love within and surrounding us.

"I know this is a significant time in my life! It feels like the end of a journey – but also the beginning. This is the end of my two and a half year exploration, and the beginning of my new self. I don't know what or where my journey is leading, but I'm OK with that." Sinking down and relaxing fully into the dining room chair, "The more de-cluttered my physical surroundings, the more peaceful I'm becoming. I can feel it. I can feel myself changing. I know that wherever I go is the right place. I don't need to push or try. I don't need to force business to come to me. I am in the *right place.*" With the subtle shimmering of the moon through the glass doors, I ask "What's different about you?" Marge lowers her voice, responding quickly, "I'm more tuned in. I'm listening more. I have more compassion. I am more humble. I would willingly give someone my last dime."

After three hours or more of sharing her feelings and thoughts, we both decide it's time to close this chapter of our conversation. "Thank you Marge for your honesty. I thank you Marge for allowing me into the deepest part of your being, and finally, I thank you Marge for coming into my life." With big hugs at the front door, we say goodnight. Marge turns and says "I thank you too."

I am truly blessed.

∽

WENDY SHEPPARD
Silicon Valley, California, USA

WENDY SHEPPARD HOLDS A Masters degree in Counseling Psychology and has provided therapeutic services for women, children and families while also working in Silicon Valley for over 15 years in Sales, Marketing and Technical roles. Wearing both of these hats simultaneously has allowed Wendy to balance her love for the business/technical world with her desire to better the world around her.

In 2000, she began exploring more spiritual paths, since the traditional therapeutic/medical model approach didn't provide the fulfillment that she was seeking. After attending a Hay House "I Can Do It" conference in 2006 where she attended a Soul Coaching® seminar, Wendy was immediately captivated by Denise Linn and Soul Coaching®. She completed her Soul Coaching® Certification in April 2007 and since then, has continued to work in Silicon Valley while also providing Soul Coaching®, life coaching and career coaching services.

If you would like to experience a private consultation or learn more about upcoming classes and workshops that Wendy is conducting, please visit her website: www.InternalSanctuary.com

Soul Coaching in Silicon Valley

WENDY SHEPPARD

Both Jennifer and Jane were over-worked, over-stressed Silicon Valley professionals who came to me in order to tune into the messages of their souls.

*S*ilicon Valley is the technology hub where many of the world's leading high-tech companies are based. This southern part of the San Francisco Bay area is also well-known for having some of the most expensive real estate in the country with small one bedroom condominiums selling for well over half a million dollars. Beauty in nature is abundant in this area with magnificent mountains, lakes and beaches, yet at the same time, those who live here, myself included, are often too over-worked and over-stressed to enjoy our glorious surroundings.

In order to earn the income necessary to cover the extremely large mortgages and rent fees, those who live in *The Valley* tend to work all the time. Even though we live in one of the most beautiful places on earth, we are often so wrapped up in technology, computers, digital gadgets and television, that we have very little time left over to appreciate and enjoy our lives. We tend to be in such a hurry, rushing from one place to the next, continually trying to get that next great money-making idea or gadget to market that we miss seeing the beauty in the people with whom we interact, or in the abundance of nature all around us.

We work while at work, we work at home on personal to-do's, and large numbers of people also work from home. While it sounds like heaven to be able to work at home in your pajamas, anyone who's done this knows that you end up putting in more hours working from home than if you had traveled into the office. On the days we do commute into the office, we sit in snarled traffic only to come home to a laundry list of things to be done in the little free time we've managed to carve out for ourselves. In addition to our fast-paced lives, like everyone else in the world, we are continually surrounded by life stresses that are both *good* (marriages, babies being born, promotions at work) and *bad* (divorces, affairs, deaths, layoffs).

There's so much *noise* surrounding us in Silicon Valley that it is very difficult to hear our inner guidance and notice the many blessings that come our way each day. There are more times than I can tell you that I've heard the voice in my head saying "take this exit" and I've *argued* with that voice that it would be so much longer to go that route, only to sit in snarled traffic resulting from an accident that I couldn't see when the message came through.

Living in Silicon Valley and working for high tech companies for the past fifteen years has allowed me to closely relate to my clients, since we're all over-exposed to the same noise, media, pollution, traffic, and the need to provide an income that is substantial enough to cover the very large rents and mortgages that many of us have, in order to live in this unique area. Like my clients, I'm not always grounded and sometimes the messages that I receive don't make sense to me immediately. But I have found that if you can slow down enough and listen, the true meaning will shine through.

We all receive daily guidance if we can just silence the noise long enough to tune into what is being communicated. Soul Coaching is a great vehicle to help tap into and fine-tune these messages. Your soul knows exactly what you need to do in your path, but sometimes our ego or the noise that surrounds us gets in the way of hearing those messages. Like a radio station, messages are constantly being broadcast to you. But when we are stressed out and over-worked, the signal comes through fuzzy or just plain static. During a Soul Coaching session, the Soul Coach uses guided meditation and other techniques to help clients tune the dial of the radio to allow clear access to the channel (their soul) that is broadcasting important messages. Sometimes these messages have a clear meaning for the client, allowing immediate insight and guidance. More often than not, when a message doesn't make sense right away the complete meaning will unfold over time.

Messages from the Future
One of the most powerful Soul Coaching sessions I conducted was with a woman named Jane who was the Public Relations Director for a Silicon Valley firm. Jane was under a great deal of stress from her high-profile job, and was looking to find some guidance on how to be more balanced. Though she was regularly practicing yoga and reading spiritual books, she wanted to see if she could receive some messages that would help her in her career and personal life.

Before we started our first session, I asked her what results she wanted to achieve from our time together. Jane replied that she was open to any messages or guidance that came through. She reclined back in the chair, closed her eyes and together we focused on her breathing. Since this was her first session, Jane was a bit nervous about the process, so it took some time before she arrived at the point where she saw, heard or felt anything at all. This process is different for everyone. Not everyone is visual. In fact some people just get a *sense* of something, or they'll *hear* rather than see.

During the rest of our 90 minute session, Jane became completely relaxed reclining in her chair, and began describing the images she was seeing in her guided meditation. Jane said she felt as though her head were spinning. She saw a grassy hill, a field of brown grass, and felt as if she was flying through the air.

There was a woman wearing a veil that was kneeling close to Jane's head. This woman looked at Jane for a few moments before she spoke the words, "everything is okay" and "all is well." Jane saw images of a field, a tractor, a bird, and tractor tracks, yet none of this seemed familiar.

As we began to wrap up the session, I asked Jane if there were any other messages from her soul and she replied that she felt that she had received all the information she needed. When it was time for her to come back to her waking consciousness, Jane felt remarkably refreshed and at peace and was not at all anxious, as she had been when we first began. In sharing her thoughts on the session, she said she felt that the woman kneeling next to her was a guide. She knew that she'd received important information, and even though she didn't know what it all meant, she found peace in the message that "all is well." Some of the other images she had seen: a tractor, tractor tracks, a field, a bird, and the feeling of flying were all things that didn't make sense to Jane at the time. She left the session feeling confident that they would reveal their meaning over time.

Several weeks after our session, Jane was far from home at a yoga retreat with a friend where they had decided to participate in a horseback riding activity. Not far into the ride, Jane found herself in a field guiding her horse along a trail of tractor tracks. The next thing she knew, her horse started bucking after being spooked by a wild turkey. Before she could react, she was thrown from the horse. She landed flat on her back in the field and knew immediately that she was hurt very badly. She had fractured several ribs and punctured her lung in the fall. The paramedics arrived and needed to strap her to a backboard in the middle of the field before loading her into the ambulance and taking her to the hospital. During this extremely painful and frightening experience, she remembered vividly our Soul Coaching session and heard the words of her spirit guide repeating the messages "everything is okay" and "all is well." In her time of immense pain and fear, a feeling of peace and serenity washed over her. Jane told me that she didn't know how she would have survived this ordeal if we had not had been for our Soul Coaching session before her accident, which allowed her to see the signs (the field, the tractor, the feeling of flying) and to hear the repeated message that she would be OK.

Thankfully, after a few days in the hospital and some recuperation time, Jane has fully recovered from her horseback riding accident. The messages that she received in her Soul Coaching session allowed her to move through the fear and pain she felt while in the field, knowing that "all is well." Her session became an example to me of how we hear exactly the message that we need to, exactly when we need to hear it – regardless of whether it makes sense at the time or not.

Past Lives as a Key to Today
Past lives are a fascinating topic – one that is sure to cause some debate at a Silicon Valley cocktail party. The wonderful thing about past life regressions is that you don't need to believe in past lives in order to obtain magical and often immediate

results. Many of my clients are skeptical about the existence of past lives, but once they experience the power of a past life regression, it's hard for them to deny the impact on their lives today.

Jennifer was an Engineering Director at a high tech software company and like Jane, was frantically trying to get through her day-to-day issues. But at the same time, she wanted to explore her spirituality, and was eager to participate in a Soul Coaching session to see if there was a particular message that could help her in her desire to balance her work and personal life. Jennifer had never done any guided meditations or past life regressions before, but was enthusiastic about what her session might bring up for her.

Jennifer spent her days triaging issues and running to put out one fire after the next in a fast-paced and very stressful job. When she came in for her session, I anticipated that it might be a bit of a struggle for her to focus and just relax for a bit, but I was wrong. After sinking into the recliner, taking a few breaths and relaxing for a few moments, Jennifer was immediately taken to another time. She could clearly see the blue sky and the tops of trees above her. Beams of light shone down through the trees and she noticed a woman's big brown eyes with long eyelashes looking down at her with a feeling of love, approval and honor. The woman had soft, feminine features that glistened through the hair falling down over her face. This woman did not speak, but Jennifer felt as if this woman knew her and was trying to speak to her.

She felt the woman leaning over her right side, and the sun shining brightly through the clouds onto her face. She then saw the back of a man with long, dark hair that was pulled back with a band at the back, like a ponytail or braid. In another flash, she saw a man in a v-neck shirt with short, dark hair just over the ears. Jennifer realized that she WAS this man. This revelation was so startling that Jennifer raised her voice and stated "I'm not imagining this . . . I am seeing these images straight through and I know this man *is me*."

> ### Surrender
>
> *AFFIRMATION: All is well.*
> *I surrender to my inner guidance.*
>
> *Let go and let God.*
> *All is well. You don't have to*
> *do it all alone. Release negative*
> *thoughts about yourself, for*
> *your life is divinely guided.*

The man was walking down a long hallway on a dark antique carpet with very intricate patterns. There were windows on the left side of this hall and doors to the right with a set of double doors at the end of the hall. He walked through the double doors and into a very rich looking room full of ornate details, including a lamp on the side table and two drinks on a table in the middle of the room. He appeared to be wearing riding boots and carrying a sword. Jennifer had the feeling that this man was an officer in the Civil War and that this was his home.

Although Jennifer continued to see images that didn't really make sense to her, and her voice now conveyed this confusion, she relayed that she was seeing the side of someone's head with the hair swept back so that all the focus was on the ear. When she tried to concentrate on the ear, it disappeared and the shape of a spade appeared. Soon, it became clear that this soldier was lying on the ground in a clearing, so that the sun was on his face and all he could see was the tops of the trees that surrounded him, the blue sky, the sunlight streaming through and the woman kneeling at his right side.

Jennifer expressed that her head physically hurt and that she believed that this man had sustained a head injury in the field and was now dying. As soon as she described this image, she was immediately brought back into the room with all the ornate details. Here she was speaking with the man with long dark hair that she had seen earlier. This man gave news that made the soldier lose his breath, and at this moment Jennifer's own breath became labored. The soldier's gaze went past the heavy drapes as he turned to look around the room. His focus stopped at a beautifully made bed. What caught his eye was the wood grain shape at the end of the bed – a spade. This shape was repeated several times over the course of our session. As we were now nearing the end of our session, Jennifer confirmed that she felt complete, having received all the messages that she needed. We wrapped up the session by discussing this amazingly detailed past life that Jennifer had just experienced, and what its meaning was for her.

Jennifer believed that she had been a wealthy man, a Civil War officer, who was deeply in love with the woman in the field. The man with the long dark hair had relayed a mistaken message that the woman had been captured and killed. Upon hearing this news, the officer left his house and walked out into the field where he shot himself in the head. As he lay dying in the field, he found the woman kneeling beside him as he looked up at the treetops. The image of an ear seemed to denote hearing this significant news, while the image of a spade referenced the Ace of Spades, also known as the death card. Putting these messages together seemed to foretell death coming for the soldier.

When I asked her whether she felt this past life might have an impact on her current life, either positive or negative, she replied, "Absolutely! I've always felt as if my current relationship was on the verge of ending, without any reason for believing this. Now I know it is because, in this past life, I believed my soulmate had died and I killed myself so that I wouldn't have to live without her. Now I can release this past guilt for killing myself while she was still alive."

Jennifer went on to fully commit to her partner in this life and has reported that their life is happier than ever. She credits her Soul Coaching session with helping her to release the ties to her past life as a Civil War officer which prevented her from fully enjoying a committed relationship in this life.

Both Jennifer and Jane were over-worked, over-stressed Silicon Valley professionals who came to me in order to tune into the messages of the souls. While both of these women where open to hearing these messages, both initially stated that they weren't sure what (if anything) would come up for them in a session. The amazing messages and outcomes experienced by these women illustrate the beauty of Soul Coaching – *remarkable results can be achieved in just one session, and they can happen for you too!*

Easy Ways to Become More In-touch with Your Inner Guidance

- *Practice daily meditation* ~ for those who don't know how to meditate or if it sounds too hard, just spend five minutes a day doing *nothing*. No computer, no Internet, no reading, no cleaning, no talking – *nothing*. You'll find that your mind will wander and some amazing ideas will come to the surface, if you just spend that five minutes a day of quiet alone time. You might even set a timer. Then every week, expand this time by five minutes until you reach half an hour. Do not do this while driving.

- *Listen to your gut* ~ notice those times when you walk into a room or a meeting and you get a good or bad feeling about a person in the pit of your stomach, for no apparent reason. When you're driving and get the feeling to take a left turn when you normally take a right, indulge yourself and take the left! Sometimes amazing things are down that road!

- *Keep a dream journal* ~ keeping a journal next to your bed is a great way to capture the contents of your dreams. Spending the first few waking minutes detailing your dreams can help to relay messages that have come to you while you sleep. Review the journal regularly to see if you are having symbols (like spiders for example) repeating in your dreams. There are many resources to tell you what these symbols mean, but often you'll know what the symbol means in relation to your own life by the way it makes you feel.

- *Notice the synchronistic events in your life* ~ from parking spots opening to checks arriving *exactly* when you need them. Keep these events in a journal and review the contents regularly to notice any patterns emerging.

- *Start a gratitude journal* ~ note the things that you are thankful for that have come your way each day. Some days may be harder than others, but we can usually find at least three things to be thankful for on any given day. Starting your day in a place of gratitude makes it harder to become irritated or agitated by the stress surrounding us.

- *Practice random kindness* ~ try doing something nice for others regularly. There are several bridges in the Bay Area with crossing tolls ranging from $4 – $6. Paying the toll for the car behind you is an easy act of kindness that only costs a few dollars, but could really make the day of the driver behind you. Not all kind acts need to have a price tag – a smile to someone who needs it costs you nothing, but may mean the world to the recipient. It's best if you can make acts of kindness a daily practice, yet most people find that random acts of kindness, even if sporadic, make us feel so good that it's hard to be brought down by the negative thoughts, emotions or circumstances that may surround you.

- *Find a Soul Coach near you* ~ on Denise Linn's website, you can find a Soul Coach in your area and book a one-on-one session, or attend a workshop to experience the magical messages that your soul has waiting for you. www.Soul-Coaching.com/coaches.htm

If my over-worked, over-stressed clients in Silicon Valley can embrace the power of Soul Coaching and see amazing results, I'm confident that you can too!

HELEN MUMFORD SOLE

Greenwich, Connecticut, USA

HELEN MUMFORD SOLE spent 20 years in business, holding senior positions in large companies including Senior Vice President of Gartner and CEO of LexisNexis UK.

During this time, Helen was searching for ways to get more in touch with her inner voice. She discovered techniques to liberate her talents and those of her colleagues, and coaching her team became the most enjoyable part of her job.

Today Helen is a Soul Coach™ and energy therapist practicing in Greenwich, Connecticut. Her clients are generally companies and executives who feel that something is missing, are wondering what to do next, or are looking for ways to become more inspired in their current roles. She also practices Reiki and other energy and crystal therapies.

Helen holds a Master's degree from Oxford University, is a certified Soul Coach™, Reiki Master/Teacher, Integrated Energy Therapist and crystal therapist. She can be reached at www.LoveAndGratitude.com

Coaching the Corporate Soul

HELEN MUMFORD SOLE

In Soul Coaching terms we would say that they understood the soul of the product and had understood and internalized its mission.

On the face of it, business and spirituality just don't mix. All the attributes of these two areas would seem to contradict each other. Business is rational, fact-based and logical. Spirituality is intuitive, perception-based and visual. Business is fast, hard-edged, unforgiving and competitive. Spirituality is slower, softer, more forgiving and collaborative. Business is about numbers and results, all of which can be clearly measured. Spirituality is about how we feel, the energy we take in and give off, and the broader evolution of our higher selves. Even the words I've just used would be largely unacceptable at work, and were we to use them there, we would likely lose credibility with our colleagues.

Given all these contradictions, it seems entirely reasonable to conclude that the workplace is no place for this side of ourselves. We have largely come to expect that the strengths and characteristics we attain by being in touch with our spirit will not be recognized in the corporations that employ us. How many of us are prepared to note on our resumes that some of our biggest and most developmental experiences have occurred not at work, but through the practice of listening to our inner voice and getting in touch with how we feel and the energy that's moving around us? How many of us would dare to discuss in a job interview our beliefs and practices such as clutter clearing, building altars or meditating – and how many would avoid such topics for fear of appearing that we would not fit in with the pace and approach demanded by most companies?

Is it any wonder that many of us who are spiritual explorers find that we must leave our souls at the door as we enter our workplace and pick them up again as we leave for home? We have to adopt a whole new persona at work that sadly denies many of the characteristics and behaviors with which we feel at ease. We find that we have one 9-to-5 personality, and another 5-to-9 personality. This makes it difficult for us to be authentic and fully engage with our work, and ultimately it diminishes our fulfillment.

Meanwhile, the corporate world also pays the price. A critical aspect of effectiveness is that the workforce is fully engaged and motivated, and that the talents of each employee are fully liberated. Where this is not the case, productivity undoubtedly suffers. Where employees believe that they have to leave half of their authentic selves at the door, they are far from liberated. Eventually they will feel constrained and dissatisfied with their work and start to search for something more meaningful, where they can express themselves more completely.

Having been a senior executive in several global companies, while at the same time studying and practicing alternative thinking and therapies, I have a lot of firsthand experience of the conflict between Business Self and Soul Self. I always loved my business career, and I also loved my alternative practices, and initially it was a cause of sadness to me that it was so difficult to reconcile these two areas.

There is good news, however. Over the years and as I've looked more closely at the possibilities for integrating our business and soul selves, I've come to realize that we do not need to accept this separation of our selves.

There really are ways of deploying both our left and right brains at the same time; there really are tools that we can use to blend our intuition, perception and visualization together with our analytical, logical and rational skill sets to get the best of all worlds; and there really are techniques that we can use in the office that will liberate our inner voices and therefore our full range of talents to enable us and our teams to be more creative and effective at work. Most of these tools and techniques come from the world of Soul Coaching.

By combining my corporate background (and self) with my Soul Coaching experience, I have developed workshops for individuals, teams and companies to start them on the path toward marrying the goals of the company with the goals of the souls that work within it. The results of the workshops, for both the individuals and the companies that they work for, are truly remarkable.

It's worth mentioning upfront that these tools and techniques work for everybody, not just for those more in touch with their spiritual sides. This is important, because it means these techniques can be used to great success in any type of company and among very diverse teams. They are good fun, and yet they achieve serious and meaningful results. It seems everyone responds to an invitation to draw out the soul within, which makes sense as we are all spiritual beings and are just in different places on our journeys. The important thing is to use a vocabulary that's acceptable and appropriate in a business context.

There are many Soul Coaching techniques that are useful in a corporate environment, and two are particularly effective. The first is the use of visualization through collaging to fully engage the emotions, and the second is the deployment of Values Cards to gain authentic and lasting agreement on core issues.

Collaging, or making a Vision Board is the creation of a poster from pictures, photos and words cut from magazines. In Soul Coaching terms, these collages are typically used to help people express their goals visually so that they then focus their energy on achieving them, and the process of manifesting their dreams can begin.

This does not sound like a technique ready-made for the corporate world, but in fact, it can work excellently. Here is one example of how very effective it can be: Several years ago, I was leading a team that was doing a major product relaunch. The product had been around for about ten years and was distributed all over the world. It was quite a complicated product that was made up of several components. Over the ten years since its original launch the product had been changed and morphed in different ways in different countries. It no longer had the same name in every country, and the components were different in every geography. This made branding difficult and increased the production costs considerably. Our goal for the relaunch was to revamp the product, making it much more relevant and appealing to our customer base and target market, and also to standardize the product around the globe. This was pretty controversial amongst the teams in each country. Each team felt that they had the best version of the product and that their clients would not like a standardized global version.

> ### Success
>
> *AFFIRMATION: Success fills my life in ways beyond my greatest expectations!*
>
> *Inner and outer success is coming your way! The gates of triumph are waiting to open deep and wide for you. Accept that you're already a winner, and even more victories will expand in your life.*

We'd conducted lots of market research and understood from our customers what they wanted. We had also consulted a brand agency and had come up with a new name and a new look for the product. It was all very exciting. The biggest risk was that the worldwide team would just not take to the new product, its name and its look, and therefore they would blight its launch. Given that it was critical that everyone got behind the new product, we needed to get everyone on board and as excited about the product as we were. We'd been working on the project for several months and had been living and breathing it. It was a creative time and we felt that we had given birth to something worthwhile.

We decided that we must fly the whole team in from around the world – about 100 people. We scheduled a three-day meeting in a hotel in Central London and then prepared for the sessions to follow. I knew that in order for the product to work, we had to engage with the team at a very visceral level. We needed to deploy their hearts and souls, not just their minds. If we could do this, then they would resonate deeply with the new product, its objectives and characteristics and be able to talk about it in an animated way with their clients and the rest of the organization, and that this would guarantee its commercial success.

The pivotal moment occurred after dinner on the first day when we did a collaging exercise with all 100 team members. We deliberately chose an evening session after everyone had loosened up with their evening meal and possibly a glass of wine or two. In short, we chose a time that did not resemble a working day. The room in the hotel was large, and we had installed 25 flipchart easels and paper. The team was divided into groups of four or five and they were given 10 magazines for each team. The magazines were wildly varying, and we stayed away from traditional business magazines, giving them *Vogue, GQ, Glamour, Gossip* glossies and of course the types of magazine that you usually find in a doctor's waiting room. They all had glue and scissors and marker pens to write on their flipcharts. Their objective was to create a collage that captured the definition of the new product and also what it would mean to new and existing clients.

As we told them what their objective was, the room went quiet. For a moment I thought that maybe we had misjudged their readiness to engage in this kind of activity. Within minutes, the volume in the room went up considerably as the groups discussed their ideas and set to work cutting out the images. The atmosphere in the room became alive and energetic as the team really got into their task. There were surprisingly few questions, and absolutely everyone actively participated. It was amazing to watch. In order to cut out relevant images, individuals had to really engage with what the new product was all about. There were no images that captured the product directly, so people were required to think about alternative interpretations of the product. If it were a car, which car would it be? Which product strap lines would also apply to our product? For example, our product was pretty expensive, and several teams captured the L'Oreal catch phrase "Because You're Worth It." Imagination and creativity were pouring out, and the teams were loving the craft side to it as well. This helped with addressing the left and right brain at the same time.

Once the time was up, we had planned to have a look at a handful of the collages and get the groups to talk through what they'd done and why they'd chosen the images and words that they had. In fact, every group wanted to present, so we did as many as we could that evening and we started the session the next morning earlier than we had planned so that the remaining groups had the opportunity to present theirs as well. Afterwards, the team felt that they really understood the product. They felt that they had captured the true essence of the product in their collages and now knew how great it was going to be for them and their clients. In other words they had become emotionally connected with the new product and had taken ownership of its development and subsequent commercial outcome.

In Soul Coaching terms we would say that they understood the *soul* of the product and had understood and internalized its *mission*. Of course they had also visualized the product and its success and we were delighted when they carefully rolled up the collages and took them back to their offices. Many had them framed and hung them on the walls around their workspaces. In effect, their collages became Vision Boards, and by looking at them every day, the group stayed committed and enthusiastic and on track throughout the rollout and delivery of the new product.

What they visualized and gave energy to came true. In the uncanny way that Vision Boards always work, the product relaunch was the most successful in the history of the business unit. The enthusiasm generated for the product both inside the company and outside with our clients was remarkable, and I have never known such a large and dispersed team be so creative, effective and unified behind a common purpose. The results were exceptional, and sales jumped by 40% in the first quarter after the relaunch. These results were gratifying, of course, but the most pleasing aspect was actually to feel part of such a committed team, whose souls had truly been engaged through the process.

The second Soul Coaching technique that is highly effective in a corporate environment is the use of Values Cards. These help teams gain agreement on key issues that might otherwise result in misunderstanding and conflict.

In the business world there is a codified way of speaking, an acceptable vocabulary and a tacit agreement of how that vocabulary will be used to discuss things. The code varies slightly from company to company depending on culture and leadership style, but fundamentally it remains in place. You only have to listen to a broadcast from a company executive to realize that, whilst that person may be speaking the same language as you are, and whilst you might understand every individual word the executive is speaking, you actually have no clue about the meaning he is trying to convey. In other words, he is speaking in code.

This corporate language can get in the way of real and meaningful conversations where deep understanding and soul-level agreement is required. And never is this more important than when a small company is doing something pressurized and difficult that needs all individuals to be in alignment. In such circumstances it is critical to be able to discover and discuss the issues quickly and easily. Given that the corporate language does not cover everything that needs to be addressed, the use of external tools like Values Cards can be very useful.

Values Cards are part of the Soul Coach's kit bag and are usually used to help individuals discover their core values and center of gravity. They are cards or pieces of paper on which there are words that represent aspects of life that could be important to people. Examples might include: *integrity, family, honesty, speed, profit, ecologically sound, collaboration, the best, fun, flexibility, growth, mastery, customer-focused, passion, responsibility, simplicity, openness, truthful, realism, risk readiness, audacity, courage, being positive*, and so forth. In all walks of life, it's important for people to be clear about what their core values are, and in a small company, it's particularly important.

Here is an example of how Values Cards can help companies achieve explicit soul-level agreements: A couple of years ago I was working with a small team who were founding a new company. They had previously all worked together in several different organizations, but they had not socialized together outside of work, so they really only knew each other in a work context. The decision to start up the company had been driven by a business idea and the formulation of a business plan – all good left-brain stuff. As the business plan evolved, the small team knew that they had to come up with a brand and the associated brand values that would determine how the company operated and presented itself to the world.

The purpose of our Values Cards exercise would be to flush out what the personal values of the individual team members were and also to highlight whether or not they were truly compatible. It was clear already that one team member was in it to grow the company as quickly as possible and then sell it and make lots of money. Another team member with younger children saw the company as a great vehicle for her to work hard but also have some flexibility around her family. Yet another team member had never been happy with the lack of customer service and focus at their prior company and wanted customer service and focus to drive their business planning and investment strategy. In other words, the team already knew that there were some points of difference between them, although they didn't realize how important it was to get the issues on the table.

We scheduled a daylong meeting to brainstorm potential brand values and then to prioritize them. We used the Values Cards to facilitate the process. Each member of the team had their own set of Values Cards. If they couldn't find a value that they wanted, we had the tools in the room to create new cards.

The first task was for each team member to take time to pull out what they thought the top 10 brand values should be from the pack of Value Cards. They then had to further refine their selection by drawing out five and ranking them from most to least important. This was done individually with each person in a separate space. They then came back together and shared their Values Cards and rankings with their team mates. There was a surprising amount of agreement in the top three, but beyond that the individuals were a long way apart. We had an interesting and passionate debate about why some values had been chosen. There was genuine openness in the room, and several team members changed their Values Cards and/or ranking in response to hearing new points of view. We then pooled the cards that were still in the *important* pile and got each individual, on their own, to rank the pooled cards from high to low.

By this time we were starting to get some real agreement. There was still room for the heated discussions that followed, but we all understood that these conversations were crucial. Most importantly, they were authentic, soul-level conversations. The words on the cards did not originate from the business language alone. They came from words that we use all the time in our lives outside of work, words that carry emotional charges and attachments. These liberated the power of authentic emotions.

Eventually, by continuing to use the cards to facilitate the debate, consensus was reached. The electric and sometimes tense atmosphere in the room dissipated, and the team emerged stronger and clearer. They had shared a deep experience and could now share the vision of their brand. They went on to develop a brand brief for an external image consultancy to work with. The image consultants commented that it was one of the clearest and most articulate they had ever received and that it captured the power of a coherent corporate philosophy. They had no difficulty at all in coming up with images to meet the requirements described in the brief, and the team had no problem reaching agreement about which of the potential brand images was right for their fledgling company.

In both these examples, Soul Coaching techniques have been used very successfully and produced outcomes that would not have been possible in such a short period of time through conventional business methods. The teams involved became highly participative and engaged with the subject matter. Having witnessed both scenes, I have no doubt that the hearts and souls, as well as the minds, of everybody who participated were fully focused and committed to what was going on. By engaging their souls, people were liberated. They had used the tools of collaging and Values Cards to help them to express themselves more completely and authentically than would otherwise have been possible, and their motivations came straight from their inner selves. In both cases, the liberation of high integrity and authenticity produced an interesting by-product. When our souls are liberated, and truth and integrity abound, the sense of teamwork and camaraderie for everyone involved reaches a phenomenally high level. These participants left their sessions feeling excited, committed and high with the energy that had been in the room. It was a privilege to have facilitated such exhilarating experiences.

My conclusion from facilitating Soul Coaching for businesses and also for senior executives is that we and our workplaces are silently crying out for ways to enable us to take our souls to work. Instinctively, we know that our best and most enjoyable performances come straight from our souls, and we know that the liberation of talent and energy that comes from soul-level authenticity can produce incredible personal and professional achievements. The Soul Coaching world has tools and techniques to do this, and with just a little translation from "soul-coach-speak" to "business-speak," our corporations, and the individuals within them, can share in these wonderful successes.

∾

KIMBERLY CARROLL
Toronto, Canada

KIMBERLY CARROLL IS a television host, producer, and cheeky body/mind/ spirit guide seen on networks from North America to Africa to Europe. Kimberly first started establishing herself as the *go-to gal* for spiritual and balanced living content that's comedic, stylish, and wickedly entertaining with the founding of her television production company – Divine Redhead Productions. DRP's mantra is: *"Seeking higher consciousness . . . in even higher heels."*

Kimberly has spent many years on her own soul journey – traversing the globe from India to Amsterdam, Australia to Paradise Island. Some highlights include: living as a yogi in an ashram; working with greats from the personal development industry; lying on a pink bed of nails in the squares of the world's major cities (long story!); exploring philosophy, religion, and the healing arts; and becoming a Soul Coach™ in order to help others live their most spirited and inspired lives possible.

Kimberly is also a social activist passionate about politics, human rights, and environmental issues. She is especially devoted to animal rights and is a happy vegan!

Residing in Toronto, Canada, the mission of this sage in stilettos is to help the world wake up . . . *one laugh at a time.*

For more information, visit: www.DivineRedhead.com

The Bad Girl's Soul Coach

KIMBERLY CARROLL

When I'm good, I'm very good. When I'm bad, I'm even better. —MAE WEST

*B*ad girls play by their own rules, know how to have a good time, are a little rough around the edges, and kick ASS! Consider me a *spiritual* bad girl.

Yes, I am a Soul Coach whose own committed spiritual path has spanned from Catholicism to Buddhism, from India to Australia, from the spooky to the sublime. What you may be scandalized to discover though, is that this path of mine is also strewn with swear words, inappropriate laughter, broken promises, and the occasional tequila shot!

Oh the Bad Girl in me has certainly gotten me in trouble over the years, but she's also managed to transform my spiritual practice into one that is *gutsy, authentic, voluptuous, evolving, sparkling and fully ALIVE!* She's taught me how to be daringly present with myself and others in all our brilliant *and* wretched glory. For this reason I LOVE being a Bad Girl and wouldn't change it for the world!

For those of you struggling sheepishly on a spiritual path that is a little less than perfectly celestial, first off, I want to let you know you are not alone. . . .

My Spiritual Bad Girl Confessions:

- I've been known to roll my eyes when people talk about angels.
- I like to wear stilettos . . . on vision quests.
- I never finished reading *The Alchemist.*
- I once had a friend come "break me out" of a Buddhist meditation retreat in the country.
- *The Secret* kind of bugs me.
- I question every spiritual belief that is handed to me and have the audacity to reject some of them.
- I've sworn at my daily oracle cards.
- I sometimes get distracted from meditation by (in no particular order): work, chocolate, men, the internet, my cats, and even inexplicably bad reality television.
- I could swear I had a spiritual awakening from lemon gin.

Yes, I spiritually *stumble* as often as I spiritually *soar*. But . . . what if I told you that a little zesty imperfection is actually *just the ticket* in connecting with your soul? Would you dare to embrace your Bad Girl if it meant magnifying your joy, claiming your power, and igniting your life?

This is a chapter about stepping fully into the messy, colorful, hilarious, and clumsy parts of your life with four not-so-golden rules for being a spiritual Bad Girl. If you yearn to inject your soul-searching with more vibrance, boldness, and fun, I am the Soul Coach who's about to let the Bad Girl loose on your spiritual path.

Whaddya say we get a little BAD?!

*All of the below applies to Bad **boys** as well . . . just substitute "boy" for "girl". Yeah, I know . . . duh!*

RULE ONE: Bad Girls are REBELS

Judge: You're accused of . . .

Bijou Blanche (Marlene Dietrich): Of inciting and exciting a riot, of being a public nuisance. I make rough seas. I set the jungle on fire. I'm a baaaaad influence.

–From the movie *Seven Sinners*

Back in my early twenties, I sold my soul to the television industry . . . and then spent the next 15 years on a quest to get it back! However, this TV host with the big colorful personality didn't easily fit into the prescribed religious and spiritual vehicles – in fact, I was often labeled "not spiritual enough" because I laughed too loudly or wore sexy shoes or didn't want to kneel unless I was privy to exactly *what the kneeling was for!* Eventually I decided that there were already too many areas in my life where I was taught to play small and told how to be and how not to be . . . *spirituality shouldn't be one of them.* So, here I stand – living proof that a spiritual person can like meditation AND martinis, be solemn AND silly, be mystic AND wear lipstick. So, *THERE*!

DARE: In what ways have you felt like a *spiritual outcast*? Draw a big cartoony picture of yourself and then draw arrows to label the different aspects of you that were considered "not right" for the spiritual approach you were engaged in. Think about the ways these qualities could actually be *vital* to your spirit. Now, take the picture, put it on the floor, and completely pulverize it with your feet! Stomp it, jump up and down on it, all the while shouting why you are "spiritual enough" just the way you are, *thank-you very much!!*

Bad Girls are not so much concerned with being "good" as being fully ALIVE. Author SARK, one of my all-time favorite spiritual Bad Girls, made a declaration in her book *Succulent Wild Woman* that (when I read it many years ago) changed my life:

> *It is tempting to sleepwalk though life.*
> *To tell half-truths, listen half-way, be half-asleep . . . WAKE UP!*

This is the ultimate act of rebellion in a society that can be so spiritually asleep – jumping into life (the *good* and the *bad*) with both feet! And, only *you* can truly know what resonates and makes your soul come alive. If certain beliefs and rituals spiritually put you to sleep – that is to say they don't move you, engage you, or agitate you – your Bad Girl should be itching to go "rebel". These may be wonderful ancient traditions that have worked for entire cultures of people over the millennia, but if they're making your soul snooze you either need to figure out a way to make them relevant for *you*, or let them go. (Caveat: practices that *physically* put you to sleep are a whole different matter! I sometimes have to fight falling asleep when I meditate, yet meditation is a practice that makes me *more* alive in the overall picture.)

When I began exploring Buddhism many years ago (to this day Buddhism is still a major influence in my spiritual practice), I struggled with the tradition of prostrating (bowing down) before a lama or teacher because it felt archaic and *worshipping* to me. I went through the motions anyway, feeling awkward, resentful, and like a big ol' phoney. When the personal unpleasantness of being a *faker* finally forced me to actually ask questions about the tradition, it was explained to me that the prostration in Buddhism is actually about laying down your ego and bowing to your *own* Buddha-Nature. Now *that* was something I could wrap a bow around! Just like that, I was able to turn a bloodless, automated movement into an action that actually fed my soul . . . *Yay* for questions!

> *If you obey all the rules, you'll miss all the fun.*
>
> —KATHERINE HEPBURN

DARE: Make a list of your *spiritual inventory* – beliefs you hold, sayings you repeat, practices you engage in . . . Do they all ring true for you or are there some that don't completely sit well with you for some reason? Are there any that you don't actually understand the meaning behind? If so, do some detective work. If at a soul level, certain practices or beliefs don't resonate, respectfully adapt them or, with gratitude, let them go.

RULE TWO: Bad Girls are Lusciously Imperfect

A cornerstone of the Soul Coaching philosophy is clearing away our inner and outer *clutter* so we can clearly hear what our soul has to say. But where do you think all that clutter comes from? You guessed it . . . from the pursuit of perfection! There's *stuff* to make you perfect, *rules* to make you perfect, *knowledge* to make you perfect. . . . As a *recovering* perfectionist, I am intimately acquainted with the pervading belief out there that if everything (including ourselves) is perfect – when we have everything we desire and have escaped all of life's painful, uncomfortable things – *then* we'll be happy. Bad girls know that perfection is overrated, and NOT POSSIBLE! They dare to make mistakes, knowing that *im*perfection is actually the opportunity for the soul's greatest growth toward true happiness.

What things have you put off doing in your life because you didn't know all there was to know about them? Or how many experiences get tainted because you're obsessed with whether you're doing it "right"? Well, Bad Girls just DO IT, even if they're not *perfect* at it. They make up the words when they chant, plough awkwardly through epiphanies, and play in drum circles . . . badly. We Bad Girls know it's better to live imperfectly than never to live at all. If your yoga is creaky and clumsy? What a wonderful opportunity for growth . . . *get going!* If you're in a guided meditation and you keep thinking about naked men? Lu-*cky* you . . . *just keep trying!* If you're supposed to be delving into the deepest corners of your soul and it feels gross and confusing and scary? Woo-hoo! *Now go further!* And remember . . . even a teeny-weeny step in your soul journey is GARGANTUAN compared to no step at all.

> *To change one's life: Start immediately. Do it flamboyantly.*
>
> —WILLIAM JAMES

DARE: Wabi-sabi is a Japanese practice that celebrates the beauty of imperfection. In the spirit of wabi-sabi, purposely do something you know you're not good at. If you think of yourself as a bad artist, get a huge poster board, take a few minutes to go wild and draw your feelings (*whatever* comes to you), then step back and smile at your deliciously flawed work. And if you think you're "bad" at meditation, well that's the whole point! Our regular minds are like drunken monkeys jumping wildly inside our heads – meditation is about observing this without attachment and learning to just be with what is. Try meditating *badly* for just 5 minutes a day to start.

Of course, because we Bad Girls take a lot of risks, we also fall flat on our asses A LOT. But as you've probably heard before, the point is not whether you fall – it's whether you get up. Let me add an important caveat here: It's not just *that* you get up; it's *how* you get up.

Our mistakes, "failures", or betrayals can be precious gifts (although they sure as hell don't feel like that it the time!) to soften and then strengthen us. You see, a joyful nature rests in peals of laughter, but *grows* if we practice staying open and expansive even in the deep weeping of grief or in the messy, embarrassing dark places. When our heart breaks, it's actually an opportunity for our heart to break *completely open* – allowing us to reach in and connect to ourselves and others like we never thought possible.

DARE: Make a chronological chart of what you regard as the big disappointments or "failures" in your life. Look at these scenarios with new eyes, listing what positive lessons, qualities, or results may have actually come out of those experiences. By reframing these experiences from your past, you can actually shift their energy to become empowering in your present.

Living with an open heart may seem like a pretty vulnerable, scary, and downright silly thing to do at first, but being fully open to life's pain has a flipside – you're also fully open to life's *joy!* Some people mistakenly equate being openhearted with being "soft" or weak. To me, staying open, connected and loving in life's full spectrum experience is not only the epitome of courageousness, but so incredibly rewarding for you *and* the people whose lives you touch. More open hearts are what the world secretly aches for!

> *Ring the bells that still can ring.*
> *Forget your perfect offering.*
> *There is a crack in everything.*
> *That's how the light gets in.*
>
> —LEONARD COHEN, *Anthem*

RULE THREE: Bad Girls Embrace their *Bad*

I don't like the word *nice*. If someone these days describes a woman as "nice", they usually mean: unremarkable, unchallenging, in essence . . . a doormat. Hey, I believe in always trying to be kind, polite and compassionate, but Bad Girls serve that end better by being in their truth rather than their "nice".

As Spiritual Beings, we can feel pressure to always be in sweetness and light, and to gloss over or downright deny the darker swirlings going on deep below. Well, I'll let you in on a secret . . . even the most holy people on this planet aren't happy and perfect and inspired *all* the time . . . and if they claim to be, they're

LYING! Even the most deeply spiritual people go through "dark nights of the soul" when desperation, fear and depression come flooding in. Sometimes, we feel just plain miserable and messed up and sleepy, and if we can't acknowledge and *be* with that, we're going to have probs!

For example, you constantly have anger bubbling up at work, but maybe as a Spiritual Being you feel you should be able to "rise above" the mad. So, you constantly put the lid on this anger with a big passive-aggressive smile, trying to will it away with your pearly whites. Well, this approach will eventually result in one of three equally disastrous scenarios:

1. You'll start projecting those denied emotions onto the rest of the world (disastrous for the relationships in your life)

2. The anger will finally totally BLOW one day (disastrous for public safety)

3. Constantly shutting down that one emotion will eventually result in a shutdown of *all* your emotions (disastrous to your soul).

You see, to deny the less than desirable parts of yourself means denying the whole enchilada.

> *Those who do not know how to weep with their whole heart*
> *don't know how to laugh either.*
>
> —GOLDA MEIR

Eastern teachings talk about our life energy expressing itself in polarities, like two sides of the coin – light/dark, happiness/sadness, wisdom/ignorance. In this theory, if you renounce your dark (or your *shadow self*), then you also snuff out your light. If your well of emotion has been deep with sorrow at one point, it can be filled just as deeply with joy. We may look upon anger as destructive and unhealthy or bad (and certainly *can* be when we act out on it), but anger also contains an amazing amount of information and energy. To ignore your anger means rejecting the wisdom and the rich, vital passion that could be gleaned from it.

Our shadow self may be the side of us that we desperately try to mask, hide from, or obliterate, but my favorite Buddhist teacher Pema Chodron, in her book *Start Where You Are,* talks about our perceived "bad" qualities like *manure* – messy and smelly, but the rich fertilizer key in growing our souls: "It's all juicy stuff – the manure of waking up, the manure of achieving enlightenment, the art of living in the present moment."

So, now we know it's best to *embrace* our anger. Does that give us permission to go kick that mean boss of ours where the sun don't shine? Ummm . . . no. To suppress your anger hurts *you*, but going ballistic on those around you hurts *them*, and *still* manages to hurt you as well. The real trick is to learn to just *sit in our uncomfortable feelings* with true curiosity, compassion, presence, and gentleness – to breathe into the pain, explore the pain, make friends with the pain, and, in doing so, transform the pain.

DARE: Tonglen is a Tibetan Buddhist meditation to train in keeping open to pain and dissolve suffering. For 5 minutes try *breathing in pain* and *breathing out relief* for that pain (this goes against the grain of most meditations – breathe out the bad, breathe in the good). For example, you're lonely and devastated because you just got dumped. With each in-breath *feel* that acute loneliness and then breathe out the antidote to that pain (love or comfort or just relief). You can then extend this practice to take in the suffering of all those lonely in the *world*.

My most awesome teacher and the founder of Soul Coaching, Denise Linn, created a wonderful exercise in the 28-Day Soul Coaching Program for embracing your shadow self called "dance your darkness". What you do is identify your juiciest dark bits (i.e. disgust, sorrow, bitchiness, guilt), put on some powerful music, and dance the hell out of each quality, fully embodying in physical form each shadow quality (I, myself, am very skilled at the *Rage Dance* and the *Coward Dance*!) Denise suggests following this up by also "dancing your light" – one by one, letting your best light qualities (i.e. love, joy, gratitude, vibrance) take over your body and exhilarate every pore.

By no longer blocking our *bad*, the energy of our shadow self can flow out to its more constructive polarities, transforming chaos to calm, despair to gratitude, depression to inspiration. *See?* Sometimes, being bad can be sooooo good!

RULE FOUR: Bad Girls Have More FUN!
For a good time, call . . . a Bad Girl, of course! Yes, the soul's growth certainly requires commitment, action, and discipline, but many people forget that JOY is also absolutely vital to spiritual health.

Well, not Bad Girls . . . you'll find us out on the big dance floor of life shaking our spiritual ASSES! We know intrinsically that play, laughter, sensuality, creativity, celebration, sense of humor, and fun are soul practices of the highest order.

Often in their spiritual pursuits, people end up shelving life's most "a-lively" qualities because they all seem too . . . well . . . LOUD to fit into the traditional definition of "sacred". But, it's these zesty qualities that truly *ignite* our soul journey! Play makes us creative, gusto expands us, enthusiasm moves us ahead, laughter heals us, celebration unites us, and delight opens our eyes wide. . . . What could be more sacred than that?

Here are some of the wild, spirited, and saucy rules of thumb Bad Girls use to turn a grey world Technicolor:

- Say YES to adventure.
- Laugh loudly and heartily (especially at yourself).
- Play often and with abandon.
- Let your personality and style shine through in whatever you do.
- Use any excuse to celebrate.
- Experiment (with no regrets!)
- Take delight in the smallest of things.
- Do what you love (or figure out a way to love what you do).

The world is your playground. Why aren't you playing?

—ELLIE KATZ

Plato once said that you can discover more about a person in an hour of play than in a year of conversation. That's because when we play, we are completely in the moment and completely ourselves . . . a true expression of our soul.

Now playing doesn't have to mean getting all complicated and involved in some kind of game. You can find the *play* in simply the small whimsical things . . . jumping in puddles, wearing a wig, a "dance break" in the middle of the afternoon, role-playing with your lover, making up silly stories about strangers you see, playing with your dog, having a sleepover with friends (even if you're 62), writing in your journal with crayons instead of a ballpoint pen . . . whatever you do, get wildly enthusiastic about it! If you've forgotten *how* to play, watch kids or cats for helpful hints.

DARE: In improv, there is an exercise called "Yes! AND . . ." Saying "no" to a suggestion in improv blocks the flow of a scene (just like a "no" energy can block the flow of life). In this exercise, no matter what another player in the scene says, *you* say "Yes! AND . . ." They say "Let's fly to Jupiter!", you say "Yes! AND let's pick up some Martians on the way!" For a whole day try playing this game in your actual life. When someone at lunch asks "Do you think we should split some tiramisu for dessert?", you say "Yes! AND a piece of pie too!" If your child asks you to color with them, you respond "Yes! AND then let's go for a bicycle ride!" *(This exercise makes me giggle.)*

And let's not forget about that particular form of play called humor. A sense of humor keeps us from taking ourselves too seriously on our spiritual path. Humor also helps us embrace life's absurdities, gives us relief in the face of tragedy, and grounds us while living in life's mystery. I'm not saying you're one "Knock-Knock" joke away from enlightenment, but there's something to be said for the power of the punch line!

I believe one of our soul's highest callings is to build a life that invites joy in. Tomorrow, I dare you to kick to the curb that albatross of a To Do List, and replace it with something like the following . . .

TO DO:
- Run through a sprinkler.
- French kiss my husband.
- Watch a Will Ferrell movie.
- Wear something hot pink.
- Arrange playgroup . . . *for myself.*
- Eat chocolate cake.
- Tickle the mailman.
- Cuddle cat in sunbeam.
- Celebrate all the fun stuff I got done today!

Last words from the Bad Girl's Soul Coach . . .
With laughter and chutzpah, I now invite you to choose a path, not based on what the world *expects* of you, but instead on what makes you sparkle, connect, and truly come ALIVE. The funny thing is, this also ends up being exactly what the world *needs* of you.

Yes, I am saying the world desperately, ferociously needs more spiritual Bad Girls . . . are you ready to join the posse?

∾

Pleasure

AFFIRMATION: My life is deliciously joyous!

Enjoy yourself. Dance through your life and give toasts for no reason at all. Cherish your sensuality and sexuality.

IRENE SPEIRS-CASKIE
Aberdeen, Scotland

IRENE SPEIRS-CASKIE, B.Sc., M.Sc., PG.Cert.Counselling, D. Hyp, MBSCH.

Irene is a Clinical Hynotherapist, NLP trainer, Past Life Regression Therapist, Core Empowerment Facilitator and Emotional Intelligence Leadership Trainer. Irene is certified in Counselling, Soul Coaching® and Space Clearing. Irene is also a Soul Retrieval Practitioner, Spirit Release facilitator and Karmic Astrologer. She has a busy practice in Aberdeen, Scotland.

Irene has been on a spiritual journey most of her life. She encountered Spirit at the age of seven on Islay, the island of her ancestors, and her inherited clairvoyance and mediumship from her Celtic roots are extra tools in her practitioner's toolkit.

For her Masters Dissertation in Psychology, Irene researched Emotional Intelligence and Effective Leadership. She is currently studying Deep Memory Processing with Roger Woolger, Ph.D. and writing a film script called *Sleeping Partners*, about a 17th century Scottish highland clan whose descendants meet up in the present day.

She has been fortunate to train with world recognized leaders in holistic, spiritual, physical and emotional health, and brings this learning to her practice. Irene's approach to life and work has been called intuitive, with fine sensitivity and deep awareness; bringing joy and laughter along the way. Irene holds only the best intentions, and sees service as part and parcel of her life. She loves dancing, the arts and ceremonial gatherings, and has a close affinity with animals.

Irene Speirs-Caskie delivers seminars, workshops, retreats and talks in Scotland, India and worldwide. Please go to http://SoulCoachCompany.com

She also offers the Soul Coaching® 28 Day Program on-line at http://SoulCoachingOnline.com

Remembering Who We Are
~ A Journey into Past Lives

IRENE SPEIRS-CASKIE

Our birth is but a sleep and a forgetting.
The soul that rises with us,
our life's star hath had elsewhere its setting.
And cometh from afar.

—WILLIAM WORDSWORTH

A Soul Journey into past lives allows us to gain an understanding of ourselves in a productive way, based on information gleaned from previous lifetimes. This information can lead to self knowledge, which, in turn, promotes constructive choice and action. By looking into past lives, through an awakening to past endeavors, we can remember who we are: a soul on an evolutionary journey!

It is helpful to understand what Dr Brian Weiss terms, "One soul, many bodies." The soul keeps reincarnating in different bodies to grow and learn, on a journey towards its highest potential. We can gain self awareness and faith in ourselves by tracing the history of our soul's journeys. It is important to understand that the emotional charge at the time of death is carried over as a cellular memory. This memory is stored in the unconscious mind.

According to eastern philosophy, we carry in our etheric bodies the physical memories of old successes, wounds and other experiences. These affect us unconsciously. Moreover, it is suggested that the decisions we make about life, at the moment of our death, are also carried through into the next life, to be cleared and healed. Much investigation has been carried out to support the plausibility of cellular memory, and the credibility of reincarnation in western society. The research by Dr Ian Stevenson on past life memories of children is very robust. (*Children Who Remember Previous Lives*, 1988)

Although reincarnation is endorsed by many cultures, a belief in reincarnation is *not* necessary for this process. These cultures do not doubt reincarnation, and have old ways and traditions to preserve this fact. The Hindus call it *Samskaras* – collective memories, released by experiencing and letting go of any emotional attachments to that life. The Celts have the Celtic cross, which depicts everlast-ing life in its artwork. Life to the Celts is a continuous wheel of many births and deaths, and rebirth. Reincarnation has been at the core of various religions for hundreds of years.

Prominent people such as Plato, Jung, General Patton and many more, believed in past lives. Of course, blocks to our self-fulfillment could very well have been created in this life. Thus, looking into this life is all that is required. However, core issues may have been blocked back in time, so looking into a past life is our only resort. Our past life journey can be assisted by Soul Coaching, which guides us into re-connection with our soul's journey. Some call the soul the *higher self* or *essence*. Deep healing can evolve by retrieving these past life issues.

Soul Coaching is a learning process which helps us to address core issues which are blocked; and which helps us to remember and uncover who we are. Sometimes our soul's purpose may have become distorted, or forgotten, along life's path. A sacred space is provided by the Soul Coach in which we can re-connect with our forgotten self, our essence. This is an inspired, not driven, way of learning how to live in the world. By re-connecting to forgotten information, we can remember who we are. As Denise Linn says, "The soul loves the truth," that is, the truth of who we *really are*. We are soulful beings having a life here on earth.

In part, this is a spiritual endeavor. Through tapping into our soul's roadmap by way of venturing into a past life memory, we can access potential spiritual assets or roadblocks: this in turn, helps us to know our true essence. What is important is that this will reveal *where* the connection to our inner essence may have been lost. A drifting away from our true selves may have unconsciously occurred over many years and lifetimes. The good news is that we can re-connect to this feel-ing of inner knowing-ness via a sojourn into other lifetimes. The therapeutic Soul Coaching tool used is Past Life Regression.

In a Past Life Regression we are able to access missing pieces of life's jigsaw. By recovering these missing pieces, we re-align ourselves with our life's purpose. These past life memories are the history of our eternal soul, or *personal scripts*. What may arise are old wounds, forgotten talents and abilities. Addressing these issues assists us to get back on track. Accessing deep memories from previous incarnations on Earth can give insight into who we are now, and why we are here on Earth; the lessons from which we have come here to learn and grow.

Accessing of deep memories can shed light on our qualities, sometimes in sur-prising ways. If you are a talented pianist, chances are you have developed your skill over many lifetimes of training and practice; but, you may have forgotten this ability and resource from a past life. Therefore, people can discover talents they didn't know they had! In this altered state of awareness we can take a quantum leap on our journey to self discovery. Polonius gave sound spiritual advice when he said, "to thine own self be true."

On the other hand, untainted self knowledge and true awareness can be evasive.

Repeated patterns of useless behavior can block the way to our true self. If our life was previously stuck, blocked or held back, the past life process can help us re-unite with our essence. We can allow unresolved issues to come to the surface, to heal and be let go. Repeated conditioned responses towards ourselves and others can be changed by remembering, processing and integrating the residual memories. Thus, we are more able to be true to ourselves. This knowledge helps us to understand our soul's evolutionary progress, and the reason for the choices we've made. We can change the ending, accept the lesson, or heal the wound; all for our own positive benefit.

To gain positive benefit from past life exploration, it does not matter what our present day spiritual orientation may be. *All* can benefit from this altered form of awareness. The process can take the form of a guided deep relaxation where all present life's distractions get peeled away, like an onion with many layers. It takes us beyond the noise and the clutter of daily living to a small, still, quiet place within. This experience is unique to each individual. The connection to inner wisdom, or stored experience, refutes *outward knowing-ness*. It provides information that is not accessible in everyday consciousness. When a past life is either acknowledged, healed, reframed or just understood, this leads to a greater awareness of what we truly can be. As a result, our outer personality becomes congruent with our inner self, the soul's purpose, allowing us to evolve to our highest potential.

Obstacles which prevent us from achieving this highest potential may be hidden in redundant memories, beliefs, actions or judgments. Going inward, beyond judgment and fear, we can discover our true self. A safe environment allows the forgotten negative or positive *conditioned self* to surface. Understanding and deciphering this material allows us to develop a new plan for our life. This takes us beyond our conditioning, fear and phobic responses. We can then let go of other peoples' expectations and move towards responsible freedom. The session re-connects us with our soul's evolution, towards a healed wholeness, by healing the past.

The regression process works on the mind, emotions, body and spirit. Its objective is to make this life more fulfilling. With empathetic assistance, we can be gently prompted to explore that time, back through memories before our birth, with the purpose of helping us complete unfinished business, heal old wounds or access developing talents. For example, Mozart was a premier pianist by the age of five. His knowledge was far advanced of his age; a past life talent brought over.

A significant life time for me occurred in old Tibet, as a student at a monastery. I experienced great joy here! I had much love and camaraderie with my fellow students; my life was secure. Something did not feel right though, and I left the monastery, much to the chagrin of my teachers, and the despair of my friends. It was a lifetime where I seemed to be seeking answers. But, at the end of that life, I was wracked with the emotion of guilt, for the pain I had caused others. This guilt was experienced as horrendous pain in my left foot: a potential fear of moving forward. On looking at this life from a soul's growth perspective, a lesson, in and around guilt, was seeded. Beginning with my actions in that lifetime, the same pattern re-occurred in other lifetimes. The lesson was to *have faith in the unknown.* In this lifetime, I have re-connected with Tibetan friends and teachers, which has felt like coming home to my old family. Whilst to this day, guilt can creep in subtly, taking up unwanted space in my life; with awareness, I am in control, not the wound.

The influence of wounds or successes from past lives can lie dormant for many centuries. With regard to wounds, the healing process effectively allows us to access the source of the problem. Until then, we are simply bandaging over the problem, dealing with the symptoms rather than the root cause. Unsourced fears, compulsions and phobias may be rooted in the distant past; their influences felt in the present. A fear of spiders, not sourced by a present day traumatic experience, is more than likely a past life trauma involving spiders.

Another example is the fear of water. This can often be traced to a past-life drowning. Re-experiencing such an incident can be the first step in the healing process. The past-life traumatic memory is released by changing the ending of that particular life. All this is accomplished through gentle, guided relaxation sessions. By recognizing and experiencing the past memories and associated emotions, our present life behavior can change. Knowing the root cause can allow us to let go of that memory. Thus, fears and blocks can be overcome.

> ### Light
>
> AFFIRMATION: *My light radiates through my life and the world around me!*
>
> *You are the light, and you come from the light! You illuminate the world, so rejoice and remember who you are. You have a physical form, but that's impermanent. At your source, you're luminescent! Lighten up . . . don't take things too seriously.*

During guided relaxation, we can be assisted by our inner-wise, self-guide-protector friends. These can be introduced to us by meandering through valleys, rivers and mountains. Though this is generally labeled as our imagination, none-the less, the experience is very real. An open mind assists the process. Another journey may take us to a timeless place, or a simple feeling of love. Each past life is experienced in a light trance. You see it, sense it, and feel it. You become deeply involved in the past-life story as the main character.

These stories can be amazing, full-sensory experiences. In a single session you can re-live more than one life, similar to the experience of a movie, only better. Your personal movie can be incredibly rich with emotion, direction and meaning for you. You see yourself walking in another time and place. You see and hear, and even smell and taste everything as if you were *there*. You may recognize people from your present life, but interact with them as they were in your past incarnation.

Many people relay rich, yet surprisingly mundane, and historically accurate details. They see themselves in unusual clothes, wearing unfamiliar types of shoes, or feel coarse cloth on their body. They watch their hands execute the fine skills of a craft, or set the table with oddly painted plates. They sense wearing a skirt, even though they are a man in this life. The visions are often accompanied by smells – boiling cabbage, boot leather, the stink of slums, the scent of flowers, fresh hay, greasy machinery or the spray of sea air.

Yet, past life regression is more than a personal movie or narrative, full of authentic details. A deep layer of recognition and understanding adds momentum to the stories as they unfold. You are acutely aware of the meaning of the past life from a super conscious state. In this unique state of awareness, from a safe place within, you can release negative feelings and physical sensations which no longer serve you in the present.

Most people experience a feeling that something has changed after a past life journey. The process re-connects us with who we truly are: unique and developing souls all working within a collective unconscious that knows no separation. There can be a feeling of timelessness and continuity; as if everything is happening simultaneously, but still relaxed and focused . . . a drifting into time gone by . . . a feeling of connection to our ancestry. This is very healing, and nothing is considered incorrect on our past life journey. There is no right or wrong way of connecting to our inner knowing-ness.

This work is even more effective when we can put aside our fears, doubts and criticism. This enables us to journey into our innermost reaches of the self, via the unconscious mind. Within our unconscious mind, we can access our karmic storehouse of wisdom and past experiences. This part of our psychological self could be analogous to a computer with its vast store of data. These stored experiences may have lain dormant over hundred of years, but are triggered by a present day event. The unconscious mind is the soul's storehouse. However, the unconscious mind will only reveal what is needed and true at this present moment in time. As Denise states, "The soul loves the truth." This is very powerful for the individual self, in the immediate moment of each session.

In the regression we will only travel to the life that affects us the most in the present. Unconscious memories from that life can carry an energetic charge that continues to affect us now. These might be things left undone, such as, a vow taken, or accomplishments begun, but interrupted. Failures, mistakes, successes: all can be buried in unconscious past life memories. We may have hurt someone; now, we are in emotional debt to that person. Experiences which contain guilt, gratitude, traumatic and sudden deaths, wisdom, and love can all play a part in our individual past life scenario.

These patterns can affect our relationships, behaviors, motivations, and even our physical bodies and health, either for good or ill. For example, someone who has breathing problems may have died in a previous incarnation through choking. Yet positive patterns can feed talents, bestow wisdom, influence tastes, and energize life purpose. Negative memory patterns fuel anger, fear and compulsive behavior, cloud judgment and impede our way.

By making these memories conscious, we can release the patterns that no longer serve us. This frees us to live more fully in the present. Beneficial patterns can be reinforced; negative patterns neutralized. For example, personal relationships may be embroiled in power struggles rather than the enjoyment of each other's company. Do you feel as though you may have been together before? Is it difficult to leave, without knowing why? By exploring a past life, you may discover that you have repeated a behavior pattern and have attracted a similar situation. Maybe the roles were reversed; now you have unfinished business to attend to, with the present person. New ways to approach your relationship can be gleaned, healed and resolved. Another example is being overweight from a very early age. You may have starved to death in a previous life. Now, you are just making sure *that* will never happen again by compulsively overeating. The session can help you re-address and heal these memories.

Memories which have been carried down through incarnations can be very uplifting. In each session the recall is under our complete control. If need be, we can awaken from the guided deep relaxation state at anytime. In this semi-sleep state, it can feel like we are slipping from our body's physical form: as if traveling in the spiritual state between lives; perhaps even sensing and feeling the energy of heaven. You get a glimpse of that which you truly are: a soul learning and growing through different incarnations. Some people dialogue with deceased relatives, and are left with a profound sense of having made genuine contact with a loved one. This may assist in removing the fear of physical death. During a past life journey we may meet old relations, an ancestor or even an animal guide who acts as a way-shower to our inner wisdom; our essence.

Our relationships, experiences and endeavors, in part, help us to develop our essence. Most likely, our strongest friendships today may have begun long before we were born. For instance, brothers or sisters, sharing happy lifetimes in a peaceful village, may now be best friends. To advance our learning, we may have made sacred contracts with certain people to assist us in specific areas, such as, humility. This pre-birth contract may have been made with someone with whom, in other lives, you fought or participated in wars together. Perhaps you rescued each other from fire and are now here for each other again, to celebrate life's loves and joys, happy to assist in this incarnation!

It is said, "The ones who love us the most have agreed [with a little insistence on our part] to teach us the least sought-after learning." Sometimes, our present day enemies are such people. They have the *not so popular* job of bringing to our awareness the blind and dysfunctional side of our nature; allowing us to contemplate issues such as forgiveness. A variety of issues can be rooted in past-life situations and choices. For example, core beliefs such as "No one loves me!" may be addressed. Recall of these previous events and decisions can be extremely useful as part of the overall process of healing, increasing awareness and cultivating new attitudes.

The issues addressed are always the ones influencing this incarnation. Time is allowed for healing and releasing of any unfinished business. All is manageable and safe. This is not a painful process. It may feel uncomfortable at times, but never more than if one were watching one's soul's life script being performed live on a television screen. We feel moved or touched by the characters; sometimes choosing to let the feelings rise to the surface; at other times, choosing to be a witness. The aim is to understand, let go of and be free from unhelpful past conditioning.

Maybe, we have forgotten how to be ourselves in a world full of role-playing. We become, for example, the person who can accomplish the most, the quickest (impatience may be detrimental to us). On whose criterion must we become the quickest? This type of life-action behavior can become ingrained. We can lose sight of the essence and of who we really are.

The Soul Coach is a willing catalyst, there to assist and inspire, not to direct, as we find out true path. Evolving and transforming our soul's journey leads to increased understanding. We become aware of, and are guided by, our own inner knowing-ness. The realization that inner happiness is not a commodity to be purchased or craved outside of ourselves, withdraws the yearning for happiness outside of oneself. Tapping into the soul's evolutionary journey allows us to re-connect with something solid and strong: our inner, wise self. We experience a profound connection to life and a fearless understanding of death.

As a result of the calm encouragement of these Soul Journeying experiences, our inner self, now clutter free, becomes congruent with our outer self. It is then that we can fulfill our hearts' desires and begin to live in harmony with our true needs. We learn to live by following our heart, mind and soul. Joseph Campbell referred to this as "learning how to live in this world."

Soul Coaches trained by Denise Linn truly have their hearts in this work. They've all been inspired by their own Soul Journeys, experienced first hand through Denise Linn's Certification Training. Denise has passed down to her students all of her wisdom and skill in the art of "remembering who we are," gained from rich experience with master teachers all around the world. We are blessed to have the source of such inspiration passed down from generation to generation.

By discovering our past lives through Soul Coaching, we gain the courage, initiative and enthusiasm to discover our *true self*; to remember who we are.

∽

P.W. SERVAIS
Thailand and Congo, Africa

P.W. Servais aka Oi Servais is the author of *What is your Buddha*, a practical spiritual book about legends, essence and placement of Buddha images. Growing up in northeastern Thailand, her daily life was infused with traditional Buddhist practices such as morning and evening chanting, daily alm giving and meditation; including various luminous and elaborated Buddhist-Thai ceremonies and festivals throughout the year.

Her physical spiritual anchor and sanctuary has always been the family's Buddha prayer room, where her father daily chanted traditional Buddhist Pali verse. She has grown up with this verse and it has become her heartbeat.

Oi has traveled far from home to study, marry and have a family on the west coast of the USA. Here she missed all her traditions, without being aware that this was part of her life's journey. For it was in the West that she encountered updated styles of Buddhist chanting and meditation. These experiences lead her to attend a variety of systematic meditation retreats, particularly the Maha Satipatthan verse retreats she attends in California.

While following Denise Linn's 28 days Soul Coaching® system, Oi noticed parallels between Soul Coaching® and the first part of Maha Satipatthan verse, focusing on each element. She sees the benefit of spending time on each element as a way to receive profound messages from the soul. Discovering Soul Coaching® has been another blessing of her life journey. Together with her rich luminescent traditional Buddhist background, she feels compelled to share this valuable experience with others. Contact Oi at www.BouddhaLady.com

Soul Coaching and
the Maha Satipathan Sutta

P.W. SERVAIS

Do not dwell in the past
Do not dream of the future
Concentrate the mind in the present moment.

—BUDDHA

Growing up in a traditional Buddhist household in northeastern Thailand, it is our belief that being born human is a privilege. The chance to come back on earth as a human is one in a million. The human body contains the soul called *Vinyan*. Together, *Vinyan* and the body can be used to permanently liberate one from suffering. Only a human being can make this effort to liberate oneself, to reach the ultimate bliss which is *Nibbana*, a state of no suffering, of ultimate emptiness according to Buddhism. This privilege is believed to be far greater when born as human and into the Buddhist way of life.

Thus, being surrounded by Buddhist tradition from the day I first opened my eyes here on this earth, I can't help but consider myself lucky, blessed and privileged. But how do I step up to the plate and walk the path? What are the practical steps to take advantage of this privilege? How do I make choices that really make my life work and do whatever it is that I am here to do? If, according to our general traditional belief, the human body and soul, or *Vinyan*, is to be the only tool available in this world capable of refining itself to liberate the person from suffering, then the first task to undertake should be to get connected with the soul (*Vinyan*).

Reaching into the *Vinyan* and trying to extract the genuine life message from it is, I believe, the task and duty of every human being. After that inner search is completed, one can make all the necessary choices for the rest of one's life, based on these initial decisions. When you find the accurate life mission, as well as your life direction from the soul, the journey becomes clear, meaningful and bliss-filled. Each mission and those directions are very unique, depending on our previous deeds, following the law of cause and effect or the law of karma.

The concept of past lives, reincarnation and *Vinyan* is very common in our tradition. I was born with a little red mark (*pan*) under the right heel. The Elder in our family attempted to interpret this *pan*. "She must have been 'so and so' coming back into our family," she commented, examining the red mark on my heel. These traits were further revealed in the kinds of food I liked and my inclination to sit for long hours in front of our household shrine. Although the Elder was not able to exactly identify the person I had been, she was able to clearly identify my past incarnation as an Ancestor who was a male, definitely not female.

My interests in going to meditation retreats and enjoying talking with the monks and chanting Pali verses at a young age further interested the Elder. This made her certain that the Ancestor I had been was a monk, who had most likely spent his life studying in an Ashram or a temple, learning the Sutta, leaving his ordinary life as a householder very early on in that life, because he saw no meaning in pursuing his time on mundane duties. All of these were indications of who I might have been, or how I might have developed in my previous life. This was the world of my childhood which, to some extent, I consider my past life or a previous chapter of my life.

The next phase of my life took place in the Western world, where it was not very common to discuss anything about past lives or *Vinyan*. The majority of people in my immediate surroundings were more pre-occupied with practical aspects of life like shopping, and earning professional degrees in order to climb the economic ladder, or driving themselves and their kids back and forth to various destinations. They were reaching for goals which were predominantly financial goals and just running all the time, rather than spending time finding out about one's soul or exactly what one's true meaning is for this life. While I was busy with this part of my life, gathering professional degrees, earning a living and reaching goals, my mother passed away.

I wanted to make a major merit (honor) for my mother, so I went to a traditional ten day Noble Silence meditation retreat. It is called a Noble Silent Retreat because the silence one observes during these ten days is absolute; no phone, no talking, no sign language, no reading or writing. After that first time, I kept going back to retreats over subsequent years until I was eligible for the next step of the retreat, where they allow you to read and chant the Pali text. The Pali verse consists of chanting Buddhist prayers, but these prayers are chanted in the Pali language, equivalent to mantra chanting in Sanskrit.

The text and chant in question is the Maha Satipathan Sutta. It really opened my eyes about the human body (*Gaia*) and soul (*Vinyan*). I was able to learn from and experience the profound meaning of each intricate part of the human form, which when put together, is collectively known as the whole human-being-system. Each time I hear the chanting of this Sutta I realize the privilege of being born human. How lucky and privileged we are to have these tools and faculties available to us to develop and further cultivate our quest in this life! Having an opportunity to be in a quiet, serene setting, studying the Maha Satipathan Sutta together with the practice of deep meditation, I realized for the first time the immense capacity of a human being to develop and refine one's faculties, using the body as a vehicle, to experience further and further the ultimate truth eventually to be liberated.

A new life phase began for me after moving to Africa; yet another episode in my life. Life in Africa reminds me daily of my two previous lives – one in Thailand and one in the United States. I am a somewhat contemporary person in this age of computers and digital technology, living a parallel lifestyle with the long forgotten centuries, in harmony with the rhythm of sunrise and sunset, and using charcoal for my cooking and ironing. From my African city, I can send and receive messages from different parts of the world via high speed Internet. But I am surrounded by a majority of people who have never had electricity or running water, let alone electronics and digital technology.

I am somehow reminded of the early days of my youth, the life I lived a long time ago in Thailand, before all the technology became part of my everyday life. We were used to charcoal-filled irons to press our clothes; we arose at day break with the crow of the rooster and retired to bed at sunset. Now I live that kind of life again, in order to learn from it. What I did not learn that first time, I now have a chance to experience again. My soul never forgets the truth, the basics or the essentials. There is always an imprint in my soul, remembering the simple lifestyle before all the color televisions, hi-speed Internet, electricity and running water became an everyday habit. I have had the on-going opportunity of experiencing these differences in many varied parts of the world, and also in the different stages of my lifetime on this earth. These experiences almost seem to have taken place in different worlds, different lifetimes, different bodies, even though I know that they are all the experience of the same *Vinyan*.

As a Buddhist, we believe in different realms of existence which are somewhat comparable to Heaven, Earth and Hell. But the Heaven realm, for example, consists of seven steps of Heaven, with a different lifestyle with each step. In each step there are different foods, different smells or aromas, different plants, different ways of communication and traveling. For example, in one of the Heaven realms called *Sukawadee* there are none of the foods that we have here in our Human realm. Whenever the being in this realm is hungry or thirsty, just the thought

> ## Impeccability
>
> *AFFIRMATION: I am impeccable in my thought, word, and deed.*
>
> *Now is the time to be impeccable in your responsibilities, relationships, and home environment. Gather your discipline and integrity around you like a sacred cloak. No matter what it takes, maintain your power, intent, and focus. Pay attention to details.*

of nourishment will make that being full and satisfied, without having to eat or drink. There is no kitchen, no cooking, no shopping, and no clean-up like we normally have in our Human realm.

The Hell realm also consists of many different steps, with a different lifestyle in each of them. Besides the various steps of the Heaven realm and Hell realm, there are several realms of existence in between, such as the Human realm, Plant realm, Animal realm, Deva realm, and Bhrama realm – again each with a different lifestyle. We generally experience these various realms everyday. The Animal and the Plant realm are the most obvious. For example – dog, cat, dolphin, sea turtle, cherry tree and grape vine all exist in a different lifestyle. They have their own system and experience of existence: growing, communication, traveling, breathing, eating and resting. While I have experienced each continent on this earth with their different lifestyles like Africa, Europe, Asia and the United States, I feel that I have actually experienced travel from realm to realm, with so many different styles of existence. In the Human realm, since I first sank into the depths of the Maha Satipathan Sutta from that long ago retreat, I find the reflection of this truth everywhere, both within my own body and out in nature.

But I am a mother of three and an ordinary householder. What can I do that will be congruent with my soul, so that I can continue to perform my duties and still be liberated at some point? When I leave the retreat area, I do not have the support of all the encouraging like-minded *Sangha*; rather, I am back in the raw, real world. At a time when I was very well integrated into the Californian lifestyle, with its own unique style of this particular realm of existence, my soul lead me to Denise Linn's Soul Coaching Program.

I had been a student of Denise's a few years earlier, for Interior Alignment (IA) and Master Teacher of Interior Alignment Certifications (MTIA), learning to practice and teach Seven Star Blessing Space Clearing and Feng Shui. I know deep down why the universe placed me in California to meet Denise and continue on to study IA and MTIA. It was to advance my understanding of another Spiritual life practice. Soul Coaching seemed to be the next natural step to take, after all of the wonderful clearing that had occurred in my life after the two previous wonderful, intensive trainings with her.

It seemed only natural that this Soul Coaching course would take place in Thailand, the original land of my birth. And so far, the class I attended in Thailand has been the only one Denise has taught there. The symbol of this full circle of my existence truly became reality as the final certificates for this Soul Coaching course were being given out to us on Doi Suthep, a very famous Buddhist golden shrine, where the holy relics of the Buddha are believed to be in the golden pagoda, on the high land of Mt. Doi Suthep.

It was here that I experienced the profound and powerful connection of my body with the earth. I experienced this connection even more deeply, surrounded by all my fellow Soul Coaching participants, and the powerful and loving presence of Denise. It felt as if I were in another retreat of a completely different style. The result was almost identical to what I experienced at the Noble Silent retreat. Although they are so very different, I felt a similar deep connection with nature, to my homeland, to all the members of our group, and most of all to my *Vinyan*, my soul. As if for the first time, I realized deep down that a human being can become deeply connected to other beings, whether it is another human being in the same realm, or other beings in different realm like plants, animals, or devas. I stood with the full understanding that only when we have a deep connection with the soul first, can the soul, thus connected, transcend all systems and all means of communication between the different realms.

Within the design of Soul Coaching, for ordinary people, with mundane responsibilities like myself, I was able to see the parallel between the Satipathan and Soul Coaching. The Soul Coaching program goes into each natural element in our body and even further into Nature. Both deal with each element, and these four elements can all be identified within Nature and our bodies, which are contained within the ever eternal soul. This system is created to channel individuals like myself, into getting back to our soul, to listen and discover the long lost imprint, memory or story of our own truth, which is beautiful, majestic and unique. In fact it is our very essence. It is luminescence beyond words. From this soul space we are brought back into the world of form, in order to take whatever action or steps will lead us back to our soul action, which agrees with our deepest essence.

Using the elements of earth, water, fire and air which are contained in our body as well as in every living being in nature, as Soul Coaches we walk our students through the elements to explore and align with their inner Spiritual life, then bring this into alignment with their outer lives.

- *Earth* ~ anything that is solid in the body, like bone or teeth.

- *Water* ~ anything that is liquid and fluid in the body like blood, salvia, puss or urine.

- *Fire* ~ the heat or warmth in the body such as the digestive system, combustion system that converts food into energy and moves it around the body.

- *Air* ~ the breath, life force, wind, respiration, that regulates the temperature of the body, also known as *chi* or *prana*.

Air and Fire are the elements that convert the other elements into energy that move the whole system into action. Without these two elements, the body or anything else becomes lifeless.

These elements are looked at and examined in detail for 28 days, giving seven days to each element. With different degrees of examination, depending on the time and inclination each week of focusing on one element, this process marvelously leads to profound discovery about our Self. After completing the 28 days, we have deeply experienced each element individually, and it becomes clear that all of these elements work together naturally, both in our body and in nature, to enable us to make choices and eventually take action while we are here on this earth. It is all designed to lead to our *Vinyan* and into our choice of action that will propel us through life. The choice and decision must be followed by concrete action while we still have the human body living on this earth. The law of cause and effect from the law of karma will reveal the result of each of our choices and actions.

So far, no other training or resource has made such a long-lasting impact on me as going through this 28 day program. This practical system has produced wonders in my life. The structure of the program enables me to concentrate on one element for a long period of time, an entire week, seven full days. But, I can also participate to the degree that I want to. I can look at it at anytime of the day, and the intensity of the examination of each element is up to me, provided that I focus on only one element at a time, and continue that examination for one full week.

This program is like an exquisitely well-crafted gourmet meal in the Human realm, where the professional chef roams the universe to gather all the finest ingredients or elements and then lovingly and artistically puts them together in an arrangement, spread out on the abundant table for us to consume. As we graciously and carefully make the choices to consume the meal according to our capacity, we know that everything has been well chosen and will be well digested to the degree of our capacity at the time. This magic meal will give the right energy for us to continue on with our respective life journeys.

By combining the practical system of 28 days of Soul Coaching as prescribed, with the awareness of body (*Gaia*) and soul (*Vinyan*) as well as the deep meditative chanting of Buddhist Pali verse – particularly the Maha Satipathan Sutta, in the rich golden Buddhist tradition, as simple as it is powerful – a perfect setting becomes available for students who are ready to journey into and discover their profound luminescent essence.

Praise and blame, gain and loss, pleasure and sorrow
come and go like the wind.
To be happy, rest like a giant tree,
in the midst of them all.

—BUDDHA

Peace

AFFIRMATION: I breathe deeply,
knowing that all is well
in my universe.

Breathe . . . and breathe again,
deeply and often. Everything is
flowing as it's meant to be,
smoothly and effortlessly.
All is in perfect harmony.

VICKY SWEETLOVE
Brentwood, Essex, UK

VICKY HAS BEEN ON a spiritual journey since she was a child. She grew up with a mother who showed her the nature spirits, fairies, ghosts and told her about the "Law of Attraction", saying "the Universe will provide, just ask for it Vicky." She has lived by this saying all her life. Her father, a scientist and engineer, helped her keep her feet firmly on the ground but very spiritually aware!

She is a natural medium and clairvoyant, who experienced many spiritual and ghostly adventures growing up in her native North Wales, and now helps many people on their spiritual journeys.

She has a natural affinity with animals. Her childhood pets of cats and dogs were her "best friends" while traveling the UK with her parents. Vicky now communicates with and gives healing to animals that are in need.

Vicky is a Feng Shui consultant and Dowser. She continued her spiritual journey with Denise Linn and became a Soul Coach™, reinforcing the spiritual knowledge she has gained over the years. She has a very busy, thriving practice with clients in London, UK, Europe and the USA.

Vicky has appeared on Sky One, BBC2 and the Living Channel. She writes for *High Spirit* magazine in the UK. She appears regularly in *Spirit and Destiny* magazine and made appearances on MySpiritRadio and REM radio, Spain. To contact Vicky for a consultation: www.fengshuilife.co.uk email: info@fengshuilife.co.uk

Feng Shui for Your Soul Journey

VICKY SWEETLOVE

*I am now experiencing new beginnings, new challenges
and have found myself reborn after my experience.*

What is a Soul Journey? It is an experience that helps you discover the root cause of any problems in your life at the present time. Soul Journeys not only take you into the past but also into the future, where you can experience a future life. Vision Boards are another tool you can use to help you envision where you want to be in your life. By making a collage of everything you want in your future, you can set clearly defined goals. Finally, you may wish to go on a Vision Quest.

Together, these processes make up what I call your *Feng Shui Soul Journey.* This journey is designed to create fresh, new beginnings. It will help you to resolve your current problems, assist you in making any necessary changes, and bring meaning and purpose into your life.

Soul Journeys

Soul Journeying to a past experience can help to ease situations in this life. For instance, if you find that you never have any money, that your money goes out as quickly as it comes in, the cause may be found in a past experience. Perhaps you were a nun in a past life who had no need for money, so you tend to spend whatever money you now have as soon as you get it! It may be that you have an ongoing health problem with breathing. By going back to a past life it could be that you were strangled in that lifetime, thereby your breathing is restricted in this lifetime from the memory of that previous life.

My own Soul Journeys have given me amazing insight into what is happening in my present life and have enabled me to move forward in leaps and bounds. One of my first Soul Journeys was at Denise Linn's ranch in California when we were training as Soul Coaches. In that first session we were split up into groups of four, two people to hold the energetic space, one person journeying and the other person conducting the Soul Journey meditation.

On this particular glorious sunny morning, I was taken on a Soul Journey into a place in nature where I saw a wonderful sturdy oak tree and felt very much at home. Then I saw myself as a little pixie, curled up in the trunk of the tree as though the oak was giving birth to me. Once out of the *womb* of the oak, I used a palette of colours and a paintbrush to paint all of nature with wonderful colours, painting the flowers, and giving brightness to everything around me.

At this point I saw the *Angel of Death* come into the scene. Rather than being frightened, I suddenly knew that birth and death are all one; that everything is regenerated and transformed. There is no end, just infinity, as when a plant dies, something new sprouts from what is left for the coming year, *continuing its cycle of growth*. I saw that there was no need to have a fear of death, as something better will come in the next phase of growth and development on my soul's journey. This Soul Journey became even more poignant when, just three months later, I went through a *Near Death Experience*.

I had been extremely tired over the previous four weeks, and on this particular morning I felt totally exhausted as I arrived into Liverpool Street station in London and started walking to Russell Square, where I worked. Just as I reached Leather Lane market, I felt my knees buckle beneath me and I really needed to lie down. Then I heard a voice say to me *"Keep going, you can lie down when you get to work,"* over and over again. On reaching work I asked where the sick room was, but since there wasn't one, I went to lie down on the sofa in the tea room.

> ## Beginnings
>
> *AFFIRMATION: I cherish all the cycles in my life!*
>
> *A new cycle is beginning in your life. Wipe the slate clean; it's now time to release the old and start again.*

As soon as my head touched the sofa, I lost consciousness and became aware of tingling in the right side of my body and was unable to lift my arms and legs. I then found that I was in a dark space and could hear voices around me, and the ambulance men saying that their equipment must be faulty. The next thing I saw was this wonderful glowing light coming towards me. I moved towards it, feeling a sense of peace envelope me, and was quite happy to go into this light. Suddenly I saw a large Indian head and heard his gentle voice telling me, *"Vicky it's not your time yet. You must go back."* The next sensation I felt was a ping in my body like an elastic band on a catapult. Then I saw myself lying on a tropical beach with the sun shining and little golden lights moving around my body, giving me healing. I had asked for the Angels and Elementals to help me and I feel that without their healing, I might otherwise have suffered severely from this mini stroke I'd just had.

When the ambulance men asked me to sit up, I felt rather like a rag doll and heard them say again that their equipment must be faulty, that my blood pressure was now fine. I had still lost the power in the right side of my body which is governed by the left brain, the logical side. My spiritual side, along with my guides, angels and elementals had all kept me going and I knew I wasn't to give up. I have since meditated to see if I could emulate this same experience but could not. Although I am a very spiritual person there is a scientific side of me that always wants proof. In this second meditation the same Indian called *Galloping Horse* came to me and explained that there is nothing to fear from death, and that when my time comes, it will be as it was when I had the stroke. He said that I will close my eyes and go to sleep and pass through into the light. This helped me to more fully understand my first Soul Journey with the *Angel of Death*. I am now experiencing new beginnings, new challenges and have found myself *reborn* after my experience.

A Soul Journey Meditation

Sit relaxed. Close your eyes and breathe gently in and out normally. Be aware of your breathing and as you do so, breathe more slowly and deeply. Feel your body relaxing more with every breath. Your toes, legs, fingers, arms, shoulders, neck and face relax. Move your head from side to side to relax completely. Now go to a place in nature. This can be a beach you know, a lake, a wooded area, a lovely garden, a waterfall – somewhere you feel safe and secure. Once there, you will notice there is a doorway in front of you. Make your way towards this door, open the door and go through it. You will find there is a magic carpet waiting for you. Sit on the magic carpet feeling completely safe.

As the magic carpet flies up into the universe, up into the stars above, you feel safe, secure and happy. Down below, you can see past scenes from your life flash before you. As the carpet slowly descends, it comes down into a scene where you are given the opportunity to change what happened in this scene. Make changes for the better to improve your life in that scene knowing that you are also bringing those changes with you into the present time to improve your present life, and your future.

Once you are happy with the changes you have made, make your way back onto the magic carpet, feeling safe and secure and going back above all the scenes of your life, back into the stars and the universe, feeling safe, secure and happy, as the magic carpet brings you back down again outside the doorway to your special place in nature. Go back through the doorway, taking those feelings of happiness, safety and security with you into your present life and into your future.

Soul Journey Case Study

I took Annette on a Soul Journey after she had told me she was having problems with not having enough money to do her projects and found that people owed her money all the time. In her Soul Journey, Annette found herself in a leper colony. First of all she was a beggar on the streets with not enough food and no money. Then, she went to work at the leper colony where she was given food, shelter and clothes. She found that the people who died gave her their money and possessions, so that she was no longer poor. I asked her to bring that feeling of sufficiency back with her to the present time, so that she would have the money and prosperity that she wants in this lifetime, and enough to also help others. Annette phoned me after a couple of weeks to say that her financial situation had changed, and that the people who owed her money had now paid. She also had new clients who worked in a hospital.

Future Soul Journeys
Soul Journeys can also bring amazing insights into your future too. I found myself on one Soul Journey in the African Jungle, working in a laboratory. In this laboratory, there were people from all nations, but also people who appeared to be from other planets. I had traveled into a future lifetime where I was a Doctor working in a laboratory seeking to cure the ailments of new diseases. Cancer was no longer the concern it is today, because a cure had been found. There where different types of machines onto which I placed samples. These were transported into other machines to be mixed into an antidote for a specific disease, just by pressing the right combination of letters and symbols on the machine. In my present day life I am a healer, not of a scientific nature but a spiritual earth healer. I work with crystals to heal both the earth and people's homes, so it was fascinating to be able to see myself as a Doctor in the future, in this Soul Journey.

Spirit Name Soul Journeys
Soul Journeys can also be used to discover your spirit animal name. When I sat in the garden on another Soul Journey to find my Spirit Name – the word *Hummingbird* came to me. I asked my guide if this was my Spirit Name and I was told *yes*, but, wanting further confirmation, I asked for a sign. When I opened my eyes I saw two beautiful hummingbirds – something I had never seen before, coming from the UK. This was a wonderful confirmation for me! Later when I made my Vision Board I included a picture of a hummingbird which I had cut out before I took this Soul Journey. This was even more confirmation!

Different Ways to Soul Journey
There are many different forms of Soul Journeys and what suits one person may not always suit another. I found this to be true with Nicky C. She was having a problem with an overbearing father. There was no communication between them, and they had lost their love and trust in each other as a father and daughter. I took her to a place in nature where she felt comfortable and there was a door. But when she opened the door, she found herself in a black space with lots of doors. Although we tried opening these doors into a past experience, she simply didn't feel comfortable.

We returned to her comfortable place in nature and I asked her to take a few steps up a staircase, into a nearby floating cloud. Nicky felt more at home with this and it brought her into a scene where she floated down into a kitchen. Here she was a small girl playing in the corner with a cat and a ball of string. There was a woman in this kitchen wearing an old fashioned white pinafore. This person, who appeared to her to be her mother, didn't have any time for her because she was so busy preparing food. I asked how she would like to change this scene. She changed it by bringing more helpers into the kitchen so that her mother would have more time to spend playing with her. In her present life, Nicky's father had no time for her as a child and this had continued into her adulthood. Through changing the scene, Nicky found that her relationship with her father improved, and that they became more tolerant and trusting of each other.

Some people may prefer to be taken on a journey where they sit in a cinema, and see their past life scene projected onto a screen. This works well for people who cannot envision themselves in a place of nature and only see blackness. When they can relate the blackness to sitting in a cinema, it becomes more real. This enables them to see their past life on the screen in their mind's eye, and to Soul Journey more easily.

Soul Journeys are the beginning of your Feng Shui Soul Journey. They assist you to arrive at where you want to be in your life. Many people who have been made redundant, or divorced, and people who want a new partner, or to change their career, can use Soul Journeys and Feng Shui principles, such as a Vision Board, to make what they want in their life become a reality.

Feng Shui Vision Board

I have found that using a Vision Board helps to *sow the seeds* of what I would like my best life to be. This has worked time and again, by simply giving the universe my messages, though writing them down and expressing them through pictures.

It has worked so well in my own life, I now share it with my Feng Shui clients and students, and they too have reported amazing results in their lives. One client, Annabelle from Chester, placed on her Vision Board her intention, among other things, that she would like to travel to Ayres Rock, dating it three months into the future. She later contacted me to say that she had her flights booked and was now on her way to Australia. This came just two months after placing it on her Vision Board. Just recently, she informed me of her recent engagement to the man of her dreams. Her job was going well too.

However, be aware of what you wish for, and try to be very accurate as to what you place on your Vision Board. Make sure it is exactly what you want. If you miss something and do not include enough information, or don't quite word it in the right way, you could end up with something not quite what you expected. So, *be careful what you wish for.* By giving your thoughts to the universe using a Vision Board and using your intent in your words and pictures, your vision becomes real.

Feng Shui Soul Coaching Collage

A Soul Coaching Collage is similar to a Vision Board, but with more focus on the placement of your words and images. Use your intuition to place the pictures and words on the paper in your collage, where you feel they need to go. When collaging, choose all the pictures you like from magazines, including words and phrases that you feel are appropriate to you at this current time. Cut them out and get them ready in a large pile. Have a large piece of paper, A3 or larger, and start to choose which pictures and words that you feel drawn to. For example: Find a picture of a happy couple, if you want to be part of a relationship, or use travel pictures if you wish to travel the world. If you are overweight, find pictures relating to slim people, slimming foods and words stating affirmations such as *I am at my perfect weight* or similar, cut out from the magazines. As the overall picture evolves, you will find that it begins to tell a story of what your soul truly desires.

My own personal experience came with this book. I wanted to write a book and so I cut out the words of the book title, with the intention that it would be on July's bookshelf – not realizing at that time that it was July's bookshelf over a year away! By putting the collage where you can see it daily, it will strengthen the intention of everything you wish to create in your life.

Time Lining

I've looked at different ways of working with time lining. My own experience has taught me that it is not the Past that counts, but the Present and the Future. It's the *now* and where you are going that's important. For groups I facilitate for my *Feng Shui for your Soul Journey* weekend, I give each person a picture of a body, and ask them to draw in their own aura, with all the colors and layers of each year of their lives. It is not necessary to draw fifty lines if you are fifty years old. It could be that ten years of your life are the same line and colour, but this might be disrupted if, for example, there has been a divorce. It is amazing to see the different colors that people draw and the shapes of their aura. When we discuss any odd shapes, these always occur where students have had a change in their lives such as births, marriage, moving home, or new partners. The students use the color they feel is appropriate for these events in their life. It's amazing how colour affects our lives in so many ways. The group then visualizes themselves with perfect auras and good, happy, healthy lives.

Feng Shui Soul Coaching Vision Quest

The Vision Quest helps to awaken your true Soul's yearning. Though some people will find this a greater challenge than the processes of Soul Journeys, and making a Vision Board, Collage, or Time lining, it is well worth the effort. Vision Quest can be done as a group exercise where the person who wants to move home, for example, can ask the group to reinforce this vision by Soul Journeying with them to a vision of their new home, reinforcing what the house looks like. Such as: a detached house, in a village, with a car on the drive, surrounded by trees and flowers, and made of brick or wood. You may doubt that this can work, because people might imagine different houses and have different ideas, but strange as it may seem, it does! In the group Vision Quest, everyone in the group holds the same vision, and because there are more people holding the same *intention,* the message you send from your Soul to the Universe is greatly reinforced.

There is another choice for Vision Quest which can be completed alone and outside, and through being at one with your Soul and nature. This is accomplished by finding a place where you can feel safe and secure, to sit for a few hours or up to twenty-four hours if you can. Here you will meditate and Soul Journey into a place where you can see yourself in the future, in a happy, positive situation. When sitting outside, you may see messages coming to you from the birds, the shapes of the clouds in the sky, and the thoughts that enter your head as you sit there. I would encourage you to take pen and paper to write everything down, and bring something to eat and drink so that you don't have to move from your quiet space. Also let someone know exactly where you are, in case of any emergency.

It may be that you decide to do a Vision Quest in your own garden, or you could sit in the woods or even by the ocean. Trust that you will find the best place to be, in order to find your answers. It is your decision to make, for *your soul knows the truth.*

May your Feng Shui Soul Journey bring wonderful new beginnings into your life!

∾

REBECCA NELSON
Warrandyte, Victoria, Australia

REBECCA HAS ALWAYS LED a life *close to Nature.* Born in Oregon, raised by spiritual and scientific parents who believed that God was in Nature and Nature was good. Her interest in the essential nature of all things developed into a passion for shamanism and spiritual understanding.

After college, she was chosen for the prestigious Who's Who in the World for her unique contributions to aviation and as one of the first women airport managers in the USA. Her most valued aviation memory was flying her Piper Super Cub, door open and eating blueberries with a friend at 1500 ft.

While being offered a significant aviation job, she was gifted with a spiritual crisis of direction. Defying logic, she followed her heart moving to England studying Steiner Education, Voice and Music. She was the first student invited to participate within the College of Teachers, because of her ability to *live in both worlds.*

As co-owner of Native Journeys in Australia, she honored Native American and Aboriginal philosophy through retail, wholesale and workshops. Respected and honored with several names by indigenous elders, she simply wants to assist in reconnecting people to their heart's wisdom.

Rebecca is a Soul Coach™, Drum Maker, Past Life Therapist, Psych-K Advanced Practitioner and also offers Soul Retreats and Nature Quests. Her international work is full of integrity, wisdom and playfulness – all part of the Creator's healing medicine.

Contact Rebecca Nelson at the Sweetwater Soul Coaching website at www.soul-coaching.com.au, by email at sweetwatersc@gmail.com, or by writing to PO Box 391, Warrandyte, Victoria 3113, Australia

Our Essential Nature
~ Medicine for the Soul

REBECCA NELSON

All truths can be found in Nature.

In the long, long ago when Great Mystery first created the earth
When mountains and streams, animals and plants were breathing life,
A quiet joy was in the air.
In those days, hidden from us now as in a mist,
There lived a People who were kin to all creation.
Understanding the language of the earth and the stars,
They gained vision from eagle in flight, were transformed by a hovering butterfly,
Laughed with playful wolf and made medicine from bear's teachings.
They heard the songs of the trees and the whisperings of the wind.
Beneath their feet, the red earth was rich with the wisdom of ancestors
And the stars spoke of mysteries yet to be discovered.
They walked in sacred balance with the Earth.

For centuries, people have been longing to make sense of their lives, to live in a more meaningful way, full of compassion, harmony and wisdom. Today's lifestyles are producing an emptiness in people that seems to create a greater urgency for the quest for meaning. We are hungry to understand our inner and outer lives, not only to break free from the unconscious and rigid constraints of our upbringing, society and religion, but also to freely release ourselves towards a truer expression of our Soul.

The truth is simple. We are on Earth to live our Soul's intention and the adventure is gracefully discovering what that is and living it with passion!

Our task must be to free ourselves from our prison
by widening our circle of compassion to embrace all living creatures
and the whole of nature in its beauty.

—ALBERT EINSTEIN

Based in ancient shamanic traditions and developed with love and wisdom, Denise Linn's Soul Coaching, offers us a contemporary pathway to the heart of our Soul. Denise's program brings us back not only to our true Nature, our Divine essence, but also to the Soul of All Creation – All Life – All Our Relations. I originally trained with Denise in the early '90s, which extended to embrace her Soul Coaching training in 2006. What I discovered was that it consolidated a lifetime of my personal journeys, studies and experiences. The gift of Soul Coaching for all of us is that through working with the energies or medicine of the elements of Nature, we are able to de-clutter and simplify our lives, creating balance and harmony, happiness and contentment.

Through the industrial revolution and our developing *western* traditions, we have progressively lost perspective on what is Essential to our own health and wellbeing. We are taught to strive to become bigger, better and faster in everyway, without consideration for any level of sustainability within our communities, let alone within ourselves. We pursue intellectual knowledge for its own sake, compartmentalizing our lives and either constructing unhealthy boundaries or no boundaries at all. We create complexity, thinking it makes us more intelligent. We critically emphasize the differences between things – analyzing and segregating to the point of paralysis and indecision. We limit our understanding of the sacred to four walls and Sundays, and seldom experience sacred connections every moment.

Enslaved by our work, schedules and mindless activities, we fill every waking moment. We no longer know how to find silence or peace in our daily lives, let alone cultivate it. By keeping our lives full, we no longer feel our heart or hear the inner promptings of Spirit. As a result, we create feelings of alienation and fragmentation, complicating life beyond recognition. And while our western ways have brought us a great many things of material matter, our lifestyles have further removed us from our true Nature, that of being a Divine Soul infused with and unable to exist without Air, Water, Fire, Earth and Spirit.

We are not only doing this to ourselves, but to our children. In *Last Child in the Woods: Saving Our Children from Nature Deficit Disorder*, Richard Louv presents that children are so plugged into artificial entertainment that they've lost their relationship to the natural world. This creates an emotional disconnection with the world around them, disabling their ability to function with wholeness.

Whilst some of this *doing* is important, in the process we have become sleepy and disconnected from our hearts wisdom and the very life force that sustains us. We must be courageous and realize that we are out of balance within our own truth, pretending that activity is more important than contemplation, love and a deep knowing of our Soul.

Many years ago, in the midst of a challenging time in my life, I couldn't move through my repetitive circumstances. I didn't have the internal tools to get *beyond myself*, nor did I realize that chaos (or my perception of it) was an opportunity for great transformation and growth. So as an action of default and desperation, I took a walk into the woods, as I used to as a child.

I was incredibly stirred up, but slowly became calmer the further I walked. The sun's rays were warm with the sweet smells of the forest. Birds chirped in soothing chorus and I became delightfully unaware of time and my seemingly ever important issues. Soon the forest gave way to a wild flower field full of humming bees and butterflies. All of my senses seemed to wake up and I could feel my heart open, filling with gratitude. I could smell and hear water nearby. Moving lazily through the valley floor the shallow summer creek was brimming with life; insects, fish, boulders, birds, plants, the wind. Busy, but not chaotic, pulsing with movements and conversations – all different, yet coordinated – and in quiet harmony with each other. I became *peace*.

As if in ancient memory, I heard the waters inviting me to enter. While my rational mind over-chatted reasons not to, I simply and quietly walked into the middle of the creek and sat down, fully clothed, facing upstream. At first I looked around to make sure no one was watching, but then somehow it didn't seem so important. I sat surrounded by the warm summer waters flowing by me for hours. The sun was waning and I watched the bats dance with the twilight. When I stood up to leave, I felt like a wrinkled prune, but a very happy one. I was in absolute Healing Bliss. The challenges that I had been facing seemed manageable. I felt cleansed and rejuvenated, vibrant, yet deeply calm and full of love. Since that day, I continue to walk into creeks and small rivers, fully clothed and with a smile in my heart, to enjoy that peace once more.

Throughout the ages, enlightened women and men of all cultures have aspired towards the ancient quest to *know thyself,* but that has seemingly given way to *avoid knowing thyself.* We have stepped out of the natural rhythm of our own nature, the wholeness we were meant to live and have become slaves to the frivolous and unimportant. We no longer treat each other with respect and our hearts have hardened, as we slowly close off to life and our Soul's dream. We no longer look each other in the eyes with warmth. Without time to feel each other's Soul, we have become afraid of each other's differences, rather than strengthened by them.

The Hopi People call this personal and societal condition, *Koyaanisqatsi,* which means: world out of balance, crazy life in turmoil, a state of life that calls for another way of living. Their prophecy speaks of times when people will be thinking with their heads and not with their hearts. They call these people *two hearts* and the minds of the two hearts will be frenetic with fear and agitation, just like an anthill stirred up. When we turn away from nature, we turn away from our heart and soul and as we do this we also turn away from the Creator and everything that sustains a vibrant life.

We are in those times now! We are stirred up like the ant hill, continuing to live frenetic lives, hoping that somehow life will become more peaceful and meaningful. But the responsibility rests firmly within our hearts, minds and actions, to create the life we were meant to live. Albert Einstein said "Insanity is doing the same thing over and over again and expecting different results." So we need to discover *another way of living* in order to re-connect with our Soul's intention – to find our way back to wholeness.

By gentle contrast, indigenous cultures experience life as holy and acknowledge both differences and similarities, as teachings to be embraced, not feared. And because of this understanding, indigenous people around the globe are often revered for their guidance and wisdom. Their long histories of living in quiet reverence and harmony with Mother Earth are the foundation of health, healing and meaning in life. All truths can be found in Nature. It is sacred and to be respected for its diversity, as a reflection of Great Mystery. Nature is pure Medicine for the Soul.

> *The old Lakota was wise. He knew that a man's heart away from*
> *nature becomes hard. He knew that a lack of respect for growing,*
> *living things soon led to lack of respect for humans too.*
> *So he kept his youth close to Nature's softening influence.*
>
> −CHIEF LUTHER STANDING BEAR, Lakota Sioux

Ancestral and living indigenous cultures today still have much to offer us. Their ancestral lineage of spiritual perception offers insights through attentive observation and conversations with nature. They are related to everything that exists, kin to all creatures of the earth, sky, sun and water. All beings – humans, stars, trees, animals, stones; whether they stand, walk, run, swim, slither, crawl or wing their way in the air – are Earth's children, forever interconnected within the Web of Life. These are not myths, but active principles and living truths.

Indigenous people are true way-showers to living a life in harmony. If they are living their heritage, they have not forgotten their Soul's truth. Their closeness to Nature allows a continual dialogue with the inner world of the spirit that lives in and weaves through all things – for nothing lives in isolation. And the simple truth is that all of us, All People are related, interconnected and in constant relationship to everything that exists. It's in our rebuilding the relationship to All Life, that some First Nations people call *Mending the Sacred Hoop*, that allows us to live our Soul's truth in harmony, compassion and wisdom.

Regardless of our genetic origins, we are all descended from ancestors, who not long ago, walked with an understanding of the Sacredness and Interconnectedness of All Life. We were all, at one time a Culture of Nature, listening to the whisperings of the wind, conversing with the animals and gaining wisdom from all life.

It's not about stepping out of modern life, but consciously returning to sacred balance within it. Nor is it about taking or substituting another culture for one's own, but rather returning to the very foundation, the roots of our beginnings. Certainly there are many teachings and wisdom offered by our indigenous family that can guide us back to the truth such as the Medicine Wheel. But, at the heart of all sacred traditions is a humble, direct and sacred relationship with the Creator, the Divine through Nature. This relationship is not something outside and separate from ourselves, but living within us, vital to our own wellbeing, both biologically and spiritually.

The Hopi People believe that we still have a choice as to how to live, whether to consciously cultivate peace and harmony in our Soul or choose to become disconnected and contribute to the *anthill of fear and agitation*. Infinite practical pathways to living and spiritual truths will be revealed through Nature, if we silence our minds, step back from the craziness we have created and re-learn to listen and act within our hearts; loving, grateful and open.

All healing is first a healing of the heart.

−CARL TOWNSEND

The coastal Salish tribe of the Pacific Northwest of North America has a term, *skalalitude*, which refers to an uncluttered and sacred state of mind when all things are in balance and the spiritual dimension of life predominates – resulting in *magic and beauty being everywhere.*

Indigenous histories share of a time when we could speak the language of animals and plants, as messengers of the Divine. As also in the time of the mysteries of Camelot, the Sages knew the power that lives in Nature and the names of things. So, to know a rock, plant or animal by its sacred name was to know its medicine or its healing power. In many esoteric traditions, *to breathe life into something* was to awaken life and the potential that lives within. So as our breath is identified with the very principle of life, then words are born in the breath. Thus the healing essence is within the name and its nature, not as a symbol, but as a spiritual reality. Everything in nature has a voice or vibration and that voice heals.

One has to be alone, under the sky,
Before everything falls into place and one finds
his or her own place in the midst of it all.
We have to have the humility to realize ourselves as part of nature.

−THOMAS MERTON

The Elders have always stressed listening, watching and waiting, not always asking why, in order that knowledge did not get separated from experience, wisdom from divinity. The ancient quest for real wisdom has given way to questioning to get answers that are fixed and final. But Nature is finite and infinite, flowing and still, alive with mystery. Our western arrogance has led us to believe that we are smarter than Nature. But when we place our thinking in *right balance* and recultivate our childlike sense of awe and wonder, the Nature of things will reveal themselves and we can apply that wisdom to our lives in every way. That's true wisdom – when our Soul sings its truth.

How long has it been since we slowed down to watch a spider weave a delicate web, melt into the peace of a sunset or listen to birdsong rise on the wind? Animals, plants and stones have always been honest and humble messengers and teachers. Like a tapestry, a sacred thread of beauty, goodness and honesty weaves mysteriously through every expression of Nature. Nature is imbued with healing medicine. Life is whole and healthy when it's in reflective balance between stillness and movement. Without the balance of inward and outward flow, a pond becomes stagnant, losing oxygen and unable to support life.

Essence

AFFIRMATION: In my essence,
I am joy.

Find your essence. Simplify
and contemplate in the Zen garden
of your mind. Discover the stillness in
the center of the cyclone:
do what's important and
let go of the rest.

The spider doesn't throw a temper tantrum or feel sorry for itself when the wind destroys its web. It quietly and simply goes about reconstructing its creation of beauty, with the same focus and attention it had in the beginning. Being true to its nature, it holds its course. In *Nature's Way: Native Wisdom for Living in Balance with the Earth*, Lakota warrior and author, Ed McGaa says, "Nature herself is supremely honest. It is honest because the four leggeds, winged and finned ones fulfill their true natures in innocence. An animal does not attack another based on false accusations or prejudice or select a mate on false promises. It does not try to be anything other than what Creator created . . . or to grab more than it needs."

The sun and the moon cycle throughout the day and night, giving way to each other's mysteries, reminding us that each day is a brand new beginning, full of promise and possibility and each night comforts our Soul in silence offering a constant renewal of spirit. The stars in the night sky shine brightly and yet differently. Each star simply shines its light to its greatest capacity, in harmony with the others. We too could learn from star medicine and shine brightly and humbly in the world with all we have to offer, without being competitive or jealous of another's gifts.

Snakes shed their skin on a periodic basis to allow for growth and to remove parasites. They rub against a rock tearing the skin and work until it's shed in one piece, making way for the tender but strong new skin that has formed underneath. At times in our lives, we too need to shed our *old self*, to make way for a *new improved self.* We outgrow ourselves, and some of our thinking and behaviors no longer serve us and others, but do harm. Rubbing up against something rough and hard (usually life's challenges), unconsciously or by our conscious intention, offers us the opportunity to shed the old skin that no longer serves our highest and best good.

> *If you watch how nature deals with adversity,*
> *continually renewing itself,*
> *you can't help but learn.*

—BERNIE SEIGEL, MD

By simply *being in* or consciously working with Nature, we allow her healing force to free us into ourselves. We regain our sensitivity to Spirit, deeply nourish our Soul and reclaim a life that is full. You cannot go into Nature and return unchanged. That deep healing power and life force is ever present, weaving through the air we breathe, water that nourishes us, sun that keeps us warm, earth that steadies our feet, animals that guide and sustain us, plants that nourish and trees and stones that protect us.

Whatever our Soul needs, Nature provides. She is a healing sanctuary and refuge, a comforter, an awakener, a renewer of spirit, a speaker of truth in beauty, striving for harmony and goodness. Nature is infinite in its wisdom and quiet ability to heal and make whole – to make holy.

By developing our *sacred intention* to Walk in Beauty and being at one with everything, we develop good relations with all beings. We don't attend a workshop on building sacred relationships, and then treat a homeless person with disrespect. We *walk our talk* every moment, doing our best to create goodness, beauty and truth wherever we go. We experience the sacredness of all life, not as an abstract concept, but experience the Divine and our Divine Nature as a living truth for ourselves. It is through this relationship that we discover our own Soul's Medicine and follow our path in life. We become Good Medicine, living and speaking from our heart – in sacred balance with our body, mind, emotions and spirit.

> *Goodness grows into Compassion and Humility.*
> *Beauty matures into Harmony.*
> *Truth matures into Wisdom.*

—RUDOLF STEINER

We are both residents and caretakers of this Earth and yet we have come so far away from our Soul's truth. By regaining our relationship and appreciation for the legacy of sacred places, both in Nature and our own inner nature, we'll arrive at a spiritual place of belonging. We'll experience Nature, not only for the beauty and peace it provides us, but we'll also become aware of the sacredness that permeates all creation, bringing us back to our true self, our Soul's intention and into the natural rhythms of life.

We are the Elders and the Ancestors of the future. Our common hope must be in creating loving conversations with All Nations – All Our Relations. We learn from each other in order to *know thyself*, becoming better stewards of this Earth and beyond – touching that which is our common Spirit.

Touch the Beauty that comes from within and you will begin to perceive the world around you in a new light, experiencing living from the heart. Then you will touch the Earth with Beauty.

It is a time for our own remembering. We Are All Related and So It Is.

Oh, Great Spirit
Whose voice I hear in the winds,
And whose breath gives life to all the world,
Hear me, I am small and weak, I need your strength and wisdom.
Let me Walk in Beauty and make my eyes ever behold the red and purple sunset.
Make my hands respect the things you have made and my ears sharp to hear your
*   voice.*
Make me wise so that I may understand the things you have taught my people.
Let me learn the lessons you have hidden in every leaf and rock.
I seek strength, not to be greater than my brother, but to fight my greatest
*   enemy – myself.*
Make me always ready to come to you with clean hands and straight eyes.
So when life fades, as the fading sunset, my Spirit may come to you without shame.

–Translated by LAKOTA CHIEF YELLOW LARK in 1887

⟋

Bibliography
I join with every author in this book to offer a heartfelt honoring to Denise Linn – mentor,
way-shower and friend, Elders past and present and All Nations, who continue to offer their
wisdom and knowledge with humor and humility.

Kotshongva, Dan (Qötshongva), Told By, Sun Clan (ca. 1865–1972) Translated by Dan-aqyumptewa *The Hopi Story: The Teachings, History and Prophecies of the Hopi People*. Talk recorded Jan 29, 1970.

Linn, Denise. *Quest: A Guide for Creating Your Own Vision Quest*. Wellspring/Ballantine Publishing, 1997.

Louv, Richard. *Last Child in the Woods: Saving Our Children From Nature-Deficit Disorder,* Algonquin Books of Chapel Hill/Workman Publishing, 2005, 2008.

Mails, Thomas E. *Fools Crow: Wisdom and Power: In Dialogue With The Great Sioux Holy Man,* Council Oak Books, 1991.

Mails, Thomas E. and Evehema, Chief Dan *The Hopi Survival Kit: The Prophecies, Instructions and Warnings Revealed by the Last Elders,* Penguin Group, 1997.

McGaa, Ed. *Nature's Way: Native Wisdom For Living In Balance With The Earth,* Harper San Francisco, 2005.

Pathfinder Ewing, Jim. *Finding Sanctuary in Nature.* Findhorn Press, 2007.

Plotkin, Bill. *Nature and the Human Soul: Cultivating Wholeness and Community in a Fragmented World,* New World Library, 2008.

Ross, Allen. *Mitakuye Oyasin: We Are All Related,* Wiconi Waste, 1989.

SOPHIA FAIRCHILD
Laguna Beach, California and Sydney, Australia

SOPHIA FAIRCHILD IS an internationally respected author, editor, publisher, spiritual counselor and teacher. She has mentored clients and students throughout the USA, Australia, Europe and the United Kingdom.

Sophia grew up around Australian aboriginal people, saw faeries and spoke to angelic spirits as a child. Her Irish great aunts and Aboriginal great grandfather profoundly influenced her intuitive gifts and love of storytelling.

She is a certified Soul Coach™, Past Life Therapist, Interior Alignment® and Space Clearing practitioner, personally trained by the remarkable Denise Linn. Sophia is also a Professional Spiritual Teacher, Faery Intuitive, Medium, Advanced ThetaHealing and Angel Therapy Practitioner®, certified by Dr. Doreen Virtue, Ph.D.

Both a seasoned traveler and writer, Sophia's stories have appeared in many publications, including *Soul Moments*, also published as *Coincidence or Destiny*, Conari Press, 1997, *Traveler's Tales: Tuscany*, Traveler's Tales Guides, 2001, *Angels 101*, by Doreen Virtue, Hay House, 2006, *Angel on My Shoulder*, Malachite Press, 2007, and *The Miracles of Archangel Michael*, by Doreen Virtue, Hay house, 2008.

In her worldwide travels she has become proficient in a wide variety of ancient divination techniques and alternative and traditional healing arts. Sophia now makes her home by the sea in both Laguna Beach, California, and Sydney, Australia, where she founded *Sydney Lightworkers* and teaches monthly seminars. Contact her at either www.SydneyLightworkers.com or www.Soul-Wings.com

For editing and publishing services, please contact Sophia Fairchild at Soul Wings® Press, www.Soul-Wings.net

Faery Quest
~ Beyond the 28 Days

SOPHIA FAIRCHILD

Faeries[1] are real, even if we can't see them.

Following the 28 days of your Soul Coaching journey, Denise suggests that you take time out from your normal routine to embark on a spiritual retreat, or Quest. In a traditional Vision Quest, the seeker ventures into the wilderness (where faeries are most often found), to sit alone inside a sacred medicine wheel. The sanctuary of this circle allows her to go within, to a place of silence, to commune with Nature and the celestial realms. For three days and nights she will fast and call for a vision, to guide her life's journey ahead.

While Denise's *Quest – Beyond the 28 Days* is based on the traditional Vision Quest of her Cherokee ancestors, the Faery Quest I teach my students is just one variation on this, loosely based on my Celtic roots. Faery Quests can be adapted to suit your current circumstances. They may be held indoors or out, and there's no need to fast!

During my first experience of Vision Quest led by Denise Linn in 1994, *faeries came back into my life in a big way.* It was late one night on a remote island near Canada when I joined some friends on a Vision Walk[2] into the forest. This walking meditation was designed to train our senses in preparation for the traditional three-day Vision Quest and Sweat Lodge, an extended version of the Quest normally undertaken at the end of your Soul Coaching program.

Our small group proceeded silently through the trees, enveloped in the jet dark night. The moon had already set and tall trees obscured the stars above. There was no wind and the forest seemed eerily hushed. I opened my senses to the mysterious old-growth forest around us, hoping not to stumble, and praying to see or feel a

---

1 This spelling of faeries is used to be inclusive of the entire Faery Realm, not just the fairies we see in children's books.
2 To Vision Walk means to walk with reverence, quietly holding the intention of receiving new insight, while remaining open for messages and signs.

sign. Now and then a murmur washed over the woods, like a whispered breeze moving through the ancient pines. Yet the forest itself was still. The only movement was our quiet procession forward, deeper and deeper into the forest.

I was terrified of losing my footing and falling down in this absolute blackness, when suddenly I sensed a presence moving through the trees. A quiver of energy rushed through my body. I knew we were no longer alone! My heart thumped wildly as something gently brushed up against me. I could feel the smooth energy of an invisible forest creature moving along at my side.

My fingertips began to tingle as a soft energy, like champagne bubbles, gradually enveloped them. Instinctively I turned out my palms. Before I could flinch, the creature had softly taken my hand. The filmy shape of this small, wild creature now walked alongside me, guiding me through the darkness with its ethereal light, gently holding my hand.

The forest faeries floated along beside us, around us and through us. They were no more than five feet tall and seemed naked, except for the silvery glow that shimmered all around them. Their energy felt like the wisdom of children. These shy, compassionate creatures were now blanketing us in a cocoon of innocent, loving protection.

We walked together in an enchanted silence, down towards the rocky shoreline, where phosphorescence lit up calm midnight waters, reflecting the starlight above. They stayed close by as we made our way back up the hill, returning through the deep, dark forest. Then, as the glow of our campfire came back into view, they melted into the shadows without a sound. It was exhilarating to go out next morning and feel their crystalline energy sparkling through the ancient pines. Yet when I looked for their footprints on the forest floor, they'd left none.

The faery who walked beside me that dark night, holding my hand in the magical silence, reminded me that *faeries are real*. As a child, I had loved to play with faery friends, mimicking their games and learning to blend in with all the elements of the natural world. From earliest memory I was talking to angels, faeries and the spirits of plants and animals. Perhaps you were too, but have since forgotten. Faeries do exist, even if *we've forgotten how to see them*.

My mother's mother had the Irish blood, and taught me to leave offerings of milk, bread and sweets for the faeries in her garden. She said they helped her plants to grow, and made her fruit sweet and plump. These offerings were a token of gratitude since, according to her, most faeries dislike being thanked out loud.

I'd been cared for by an old Australian aboriginal woman as an infant, and absorbed unspoken messages from the unseen world while cradled to her breast. Once, while out riding at sunset with an Aboriginal stockman on the family cattle property, I saw the spirit of a dingo standing proud on top of a hill, overlooking a billabong of blue lotus flowers.

My Aboriginal companion was a traditional law man, a man of the old ways. As he greeted the Dingo Ancestor in the soft tones of his own language, the spirit calmly vanished before our eyes! I had no words for what I'd witnessed. It was never mentioned to others, since *indigenous magic* was then frowned upon. By the age of seven I realized these matters were to be kept secret. Nobody told me that spirits were not real. It just seemed that most people no longer saw or believe in them.

The child in me loved to run barefoot and wild, far from home, at every opportunity. One day while out playing with a friend near some tall, wild grass at the edge of a track, we discovered a small palace made of crystals. We just *knew* this was a home for the faeries, and every day, visited them to share offerings of food and lighthearted conversation. Each day the crystal palace grew and sparkled more brightly, and when the sun shone down after rain, tiny rainbow prisms sparkled everywhere!

Dozens of faeries were at work on this palace, and in its hidden center, we knew there lived a Faery Queen, in whose honor the castle was being built. We believed our visits helped the faeries to perfect their craft, and delighted in calling on them to admire their progress.

One day we returned to find the crystal palace had vanished, and all the faeries with it. A few pieces of shattered glass were the only evidence it ever existed. Someone had come along and mowed the tall grass surrounding the faery citadel, and in so doing, had completely destroyed their beautiful castle. We each took a small shard of crystal home, believing it a parting gift from the Fae, a reminder of the magical jeweled palace we had watched them build.

It's not unusual to encounter faeries in places where two different elements meet. For example, where a tree trunk meets the earth, water tumbles over rocks, forests become meadows, land meets ocean, and in the case of the faery castle, where a trail meets wilderness. Faeries may be encountered at crossroads, dusk and dawn, at New and Full Moons, and when the seasons change – equinox, May Day and Hallow's Eve.

Since faeries are Nature's guardian angels, every aspect of the natural world has a faery belonging to it. Wild places, free of chemicals are where the Fae are most often found, especially when our human consciousness shifts from everyday thinking to a meditative state, to the magical world of imagination.

Faeries are our spiritual cousins; they are the closest living order of spiritual beings to humans. Like angels, they are intermediaries between heaven and earth, existing in a realm between mortal and divine. As angels of the Earth, their prime power comes from the elements of nature. During such times as this, when planet Earth has become unbalanced, the revival of our contact with the Faery Realm can be a source of healing and restoration, both for ourselves and the shared environment in which we live.

Although we may see faeries, either with our physical eyes or in our mind's eye, as tiny winged creatures, they are in fact shape-shifters. Most faeries in their true form are as large as human beings, or larger! Their different elements and orders appear in multitudinous shapes: flower faeries, sylphs, nymphs, gnomes, dryads, devas and leprechauns etc., including mythical creatures such as mermaids, unicorns and dragons.

Faeries are powerful but shy, and if we are lucky enough to establish a working relationship with them, they can assist us in miraculous ways. They not only help us to grow bountiful gardens, but can guide us in regaining what has been lost – our fully awakened second sight and inner wisdom – to help us heal and restore our lives, and our world, to harmonious equilibrium.

Your Faery Quest

We are delighted
that you're invited
to spend some time in your circle with us!
Do not delay
to invite we fae ~
We are the friends you know you can trust!

We all have ancestors, guides, and angels to watch over us during our quest. But since a quest is a *time out* away from the mundane concerns of ordinary activity, allowing us to get back in touch with our essential natures, the faeries make expert guides for such a task! As companions they encourage us to become more like them – innocent, playful and pure, with masterful skills in drawing to themselves everything necessary for an abundant life, overflowing with pleasure, joy and blissful harmony.

To create your own sacred circle at the end of your Soul Coaching journey, first decide whether you will sit indoors or out, and how long your Quest will last – a few hours, a full day, or longer. The faeries prefer you remain outdoors, but if this isn't possible, you may conduct your quest indoors near a large window with a view of nature.

Find a quiet and peaceful spot where you can sit alone, completely undisturbed. Dress in something comfortable. If you wish, wear a magical piece of jewelry and decorate your hair. Remember to have a notebook and plenty of water handy. No cell phones please!

Indoors, you may create a faery altar using a beautiful cloth decorated with items found in nature such as flowers, shells, feathers, bark, moss, crystals or stones. It's especially effective to use objects representing the four elements of Air, Water, Fire and Earth. You may also include small bells, a faery statue, glitter, or a string of tiny lights – whatever makes your heart sing!

If you are creating your sacred circle outdoors, form the circumference using anything found on the earth such as stones, old tree branches or bark, flowers, pinecones, dried seaweed or whatever nature provides. Indoors, you may use shells, pebbles, crystals, flowers etc. to create your faery circle. Begin by marking the four compass points, always remembering to enter and exit your circle from the direction of sunrise, the East.

Choose a special object, especially something that offers itself, to place at each of your compass points to symbolize *Air* in the East, *Water* in the South, *Fire* in the West and *Earth* in the North.[3] For example: a feather for Air; moss, seaweed or a shell for Water; a candle or something fiery to represent Fire; and a stone or crystal for Earth. These directions are based on Denise Linn's ancestral Cherokee medicine wheel. The Celtic tradition, described below by Fiona MacLeod[4], uses different elemental correspondences for the cardinal directions. Please use whichever tradition resonates with you.

> *Wind comes from the spring star in the East;*
> *fire from the summer star in the South;*
> *water from the autumn star in the West;*
> *wisdom, silence, and death from the star in the North.*

After requesting the Creator's blessing and guidance, ask the faeries to assist you in finding suitable objects for your four directions while taking a Vision Walk, as described earlier. You may also do this to find the perfect site for your circle, if still undecided.

Faery rings are powerful, magical portals which humans should not enter without permission. Your sacred medicine wheel is also a place of magic and power, and if constructed with pure intention, the faeries will gladly bless it.

When your circle is complete, stand silently in the East and ask permission to enter your faery circle. Enter respectfully and stand in the center, where heaven and earth meet. Feel the blessings of heaven pouring down upon you like a shower of golden white light, filling your entire being, and forming a sphere of light around your heart chakra. Now feel your energy moving down through your feet, forming deep roots into the center of the fertile earth below. Feel your connection with the holy earth, and draw that rich nourishment back up through your feet, returning to your heart chakra.

- Now turn to the East to honor the Spirit of Air for giving you breath, openness, mental clarity, insight and understanding, making each moment an opportunity to grow.

- Turn to the South to honor the Spirit of Water, for deepening your spiritual awareness, instincts, and your capacity to feel joy.

---

3   The elements for North and South are typically reversed for the Southern Hemisphere.
4   *The Divine Adventure Vol IV* by Fiona MacLeod (William Sharp), William Heinemann Ltd., London, 1910.

- Turn to the West to honor the Spirit of Fire, for empowering you with intuition, passion, energy and light, which purifies and illuminates all things.

- Turn to the North to honor the Spirit of Earth, for the power of protection and regeneration, for grounding and centering, allowing you to feel safe and at peace.

As you sit in the center of your faery circle, you become the fifth direction, a channel between heaven and earth, mediating all seven directions – East, South, West, North and Above, Below and Within. You merge with the Pillar of Light, the Central Flame of Being, where all things are redeemed and transformed.

Now you are ready to call in the faeries of the four directions. You must carry in your heart the intention to be harmless or the faeries will refuse your call. Simply empty your mind of all other concerns and invite the Spirits of the Air Element, the Sylphs, to come to the outer edge of your circle. Then invite the Spirits of the Water Element, the Undines or Mermaids, to come forth. Now invite the Spirits of the Fire Element, the Salamanders, to attend. And finally, invite the Spirits of the Earth Element, the Gnomes, to join your circle.

These elemental spirits are the architects of form, pure streams of power that make up each element in nature. The sylphs can assist us to extend ourselves and become open to new ways. The undines teach us pattern, depth and harmony. The salamanders bring us warmth, vitality and illumination. The gnomes teach us manifestation and regeneration. Honor their presence and blessings on your circle.

Now that you have consecrated your space, you are ready to call in your faery guide to join you on your quest. Do you see tiny sparkles of light darting around you in the air? Do you feel a sensation of sinking deep within the Earth? Do you hear what sounds like strange and beautiful music coming from nowhere? Do you feel tingles in your body as if the air around you has suddenly become electric? All of these are signs that your faery guide is near.

Close your eyes and ask your faery guide to appear in your mind's eye. Your guide will most likely come in a form you expect, so as not to frighten you. Perhaps it is a small child-like creature with wings, an elfin figure dressed in green, or a beautiful Faery Queen. Accept the form in which your guide appears, knowing that a powerful being exists behind the spirit you now see.

Ask your faery guide sincerely for their assistance in showing you a vision. Request that you feel or hear messages that will clarify your soul's mission in this life. Allow yourself to be completely open to any revelations and visions you receive. Notice any gifts or specific messages offered by your faery guide during this quiet time. Perhaps you will receive a Faery Name. Everything you see, hear and experience has significance.

By tapping into the Faery Realm you are placing yourself into the ancient streams of spiritual awareness, prophetic vision, and connection with All of Life that your ancestors have honored throughout Time.

And did you know that you too have faery wings? Notice how energy flows into your heart chakra from a point between your shoulder blades. Like a flower bud yearning to unfold – latent, receptive energy lies dormant here. Visualize your *wings* unfurling slowly now from this point, reaching out wide, to open your awareness even more to the Faery Realm.

Your faery guide may wish to take you an a journey to an enchanted place such as a crystal cave of healing, a sacred hall of records, a temple high in the mountains, or an underwater journey to a forgotten magical realm. This is your journey, so remember that you are safe at all times. You are free to change anything at any time by simply stating your request. Your guide is very adaptable and will work with you for your greatest benefit.

When your faery journey is complete and you have returned to the center of your circle with any gifts or messages, please remember to honor your faery guide. After opening your eyes, try to jot down in your notebook the details of this journey, and perhaps make a sketch of your faery guide, before you forget.

The first half of your quest, no matter how long it is, should be devoted to watching and listening for signs from your environment. Notice the patterns in trees and clouds. If indoors, gaze out of your window. Watch the behavior of birds or animals, both in your visions and in the natural world around you. Nature always responds in surprising ways during a quest. Everything that

> ### Wisdom
>
> *AFFIRMATION: All I truly need is within me!*
>
> *The cup of wisdom is being presented to you. Listen to the coincidences, signs, and synchronicities around you; watch for messages from your angels and guides. Enlightenment is growing within you in mysterious ways beyond your awareness.*
> *Sit on the earth and allow her wisdom to fill you.*

happens is a direct message from the now sacred world you have created. This hallowed world will speak to you in symbols and metaphors, and from within your faery circle, you are sure to see and experience many magical signs! During my first Vision Quest, I had close encounters with a young deer and a raccoon which both offered important messages for me.

The second part of your quest is a time to pray. Send prayers and blessings out into the universe for all the people you love, or wished you could love. Pray for the healing of anyone and anything in the world, especially any circumstances you feel need healing. Pray for all the people, animals and situations you've known, and for all those you have yet to meet and experience. Pray for yourself, for your body, your mind, your heart, your soul, your spirit. Pray for all living things in nature; pray for the planet; pray for peace. Pray until you can't think of anything else to pray for.

After this, ask the elementals of the four directions and your faery guide to carry your prayers out into the world, with all of your love. . . .

When this is complete, you may feel like singing, dancing or drumming. Let yourself go completely, in celebration of all that has transpired here in your faery circle. Don't be surprised if you see, hear or sense a vast number of faery beings joining in. Faeries love nothing better than a joyful celebration! Your singing and dancing also helps to ground the work you have completed on your quest. This is no time to be self-conscious. Really let go! Allow yourself to feel the pure, innocent joy and gratitude your heart now wishes to express.

When you have finished, go back to the center of your circle and prepare to say farewell to your faery guide. Honor and bless them, and blow them a kiss. Though faeries may not wish to be thanked out loud, they do love to receive offerings. Perhaps you have brought along a little gift of some sweet cake. Now is the time to offer this.

While still in the center of your circle, quietly honor the elementals of the four directions in turn, beginning in the East. Silently send them your blessings, and mentally release them one by one from their guardianship of your faery circle.

Once this is done, carefully disassemble your circle in the reverse order that it was built, so that when you have finished, there are no signs of any kind that your sacred faery circle ever existed.

Now say a final prayer and blessing for all the faery beings who've assisted you during your quest, and give thanks to your Creator. Then begin gently returning back to your ordinary life, knowing that all that has occurred here during your Faery Quest will continue to shower you with blessings for the rest of your life!

As you move towards blissful completion of your Soul Coaching journey, I blow you a kiss and send you faery blessings, much love, and all good wishes as you embark on your own magical quest.

May the journey of your soul be blessed!

Joy

*AFFIRMATION: Joy and ecstasy flow
through me wildly and freely.*

*Celebrate and have fun!
Embrace life, yourself and others.
Say yes! Soar to the clouds
and let your doubts dissolve.
All is well.*

Acknowledgements

Thank you to all of the talented Soul Coaches who've shared their heartfelt wisdom throughout the pages of this book. Deep thanks to Fiona Raven and Roberta Binder whose inspiration and assistance have been invaluable to us all.

Immense gratitude also to everyone who has collaborated harmoniously on this book, including Denise Linn, for allowing us to use excerpts from her *Soul Coaching Oracle Cards Guidebook*, and special thanks to my son Marlon for his enduring love, support and welcome mirth!